Teaching Creative

A handbook

Jennifer van Papendorp &
Sharon Friedman

Kwela
B·O·O·K·S

Contents

Photo List

E.C. PRIMARY SCHOOL, GRASSY PARK
(arranged by Yusuf Johnson, Grassy Park High)
Bernadette America, Lameez Connelly, Byron Geland, Riedewaan
Jacobs, Melissa James, Reginald Jansen, Rafeeqa Kahaar, Verlin Payne,
Nicole Scheepers, Liesle van Rensburg

DANCE ATLANTIC
Sabina Botti, Bongiwe Febana

HEAD START COLLEGE
Zukiswa Fulani, Sabelo Lwana, Amanda Mhluzi, Edgar Phillips

UCT BALLET SCHOOL: JUNIOR
Jodi Balfour, Roland Berlioz, Helen Divaris, Sylvain Michel, Jessica
Watermeyer, Laura Watermeyer, Disa Yang

UCT BALLET SCHOOL: SENIOR
Amanda Kok, Angela Osborne

Acknowledgements

This book was compiled and written with a good deal of help and support. Precious time was spent by our colleagues, reading our drafts. We would like to express our appreciation and gratitude for the valuable feedback to: Gillian Mitchell, Ingrid Miller, Sylvia Glasser, Danie Fourie, Gay Morris, David Spurgeon, Jill Waterman, Diane Cheesman, Professor Elizabeth Triegaardt, Illona Frege and Soili Hämäläinin.

We would like to thank Woolworths Pty Ltd, who so kindly sponsored our photographs; Dave Levin of Medical Graphics who took the photographs and the students who gave up a Saturday to demonstrate for the camera.

Finally we would like to thank our publisher Annari van der Merwe of Kwela Books for her support and endless patience when we were unable to meet deadlines.

Preface

Changes in government, education systems and values are opening up new possibilities. As of the mid 1990s, a wide range of stakeholders are participating in forming South African arts education policy, providing an opportunity to make previously marginalised arts subjects into a lively and valued part of the core education curriculum. For the first time in the history of our education system, schools can elect Dance as an option for the core syllabus, placing Dance as a subject on the timetable for all pupils. In the new South African Curriculum Framework, Dance is included in the mainstream of education as a part of the Learning Area: Arts and Culture.

Consequently, the need has arisen for relevant support materials for in-service primary and secondary school teachers using the Interim syllabus for Creative Dance and the Curriculum 2005 framework. The book was written with other interest groups in mind as well, such as pre-service student teachers, non-governmental organisation (NGO) and community dance teachers, university and college lecturers, movement-for-actors lecturers, drama teachers and community recreation facilitators.

The focus of this book is the field of dance called, variously, Creative Dance, Creative Movement, Educational Dance, Expressive Movement or Movement for Actors. In this book we use the term *Creative Dance*. It is a dance form based on natural movement rather than a particular style or technique. It is expressive and non-prescriptive in that it prescribes *no right or wrong way of doing things* because each movement is a personal decision of the mover. It is not technically oriented although certain mastery may be achieved through it. It is a creative art experience which celebrates each person's uniqueness, emphasises individual creativity and structures opportunities for interaction in a safe environment. Based on the laws of bodily movement, it should be simple enough to be a vitalising experience for all, and complex enough to prove interesting and valuable to those who wish to make Dance their chosen profession.

The first part of the book describes the philosophy and teaching methods of Creative Dance. In line with the Department of Education's 'Interim Core Syllabus: Dance – Creative Movement', concepts are explained and examples of activities for each section are provided. The sample exercises can be adapted for any age group. These ideas by no means exhaust the subject, nor are they meant to be prescriptive in any way. They are provided as a guide or starting point. Teachers need to be as creative as their students in expanding the possibilities.

This book will not by itself make anyone a teacher of movement, but is designed to support trained or training dance teachers. Learning in any of the arts demands more than reading or thinking. It is necesssary to *experience* movement, to be able to remember and anticipate individual responses. Some of the ideas represent only 'a foot in the door' of a given area of exploration and study. They need to be adapted to different situations and many more ideas and examples need to be generated.

Learning to create in Dance follows the same sequence as learning to write; one begins by discovering or learning movements: letters, putting them together in sequence (words), adding variations (adverbs and adjectives) and expressing meaning (ideas, thoughts, stories).

Within the exercises instructions are written as if speaking to the learners and instructions to the teacher are italicised.

PART ONE

The Principles of Teaching
Creative Dance

CHAPTER I

Introduction

'Each person is his own art'
(Anna Halprin)

From the moment of birth to the very last breath, people have a need to move in order to function, to express themselves and to communicate. How each person moves in everyday actions and activities is an expression and manifestation of who they are. That flow of movement through life is one's own personal 'dance of life', an *expression of self* and a *means of communicating* with others.

In some people this capacity is developed to a level of professionalism, for example the dance artist, who communicates ideas and feelings of and to a society. In the majority of people, this capacity for expression and communication needs to be developed to a level that serves their own needs, fosters their own growth and cultivates their ability to relate to others. Margaret H'Doubler, a pioneer in explaining and promoting the universal value of dance as a creative art experience, claims that:

> Of all the arts, dance is peculiarly suited to ... a fulfilment of the personality. It serves all the ends of individual growth; it helps to develop the body; it stimulates the imagination and challenges the intellect; it helps to cultivate an appreciation of beauty; and it deepens and refines the emotional nature (*1940:64*).

Dance as artistic expression

'If we can think, feel, and move, we can dance' (*H'Doubler*)

The basic aspects and enduring qualities of dance are within everyone's reach. It is an activity in which all may find some degree of enjoyment and aesthetic satisfaction. Everybody should have an opportunity to learn to use dance as a means of expression and communication. It is relatively easily accessible in that everyone has the necessary instrument of expression available in their own body. Creativity is an innate capacity

3

in everyone. In some people it is developed and in others it is neglected or supressed and therefore wasted.

The creative dance process is a co-operative activity of the emotions, intellect, body and spirit. The emotions motivate expression, the intellect constructs form, the body externalises the form through the use of the muscles and joints, and the spirit animates the activities with significance.

Many people are blocked from free harmonious expression by their own self-consciousness. Embarrassed to express themselves through their bodies, lacking the co-ordination of mind, body and feelings, they see their bodies as a liability over which they have no control. An awareness of the inseparability of these functions forms the basis of the concept of dance as a truly educational experience.

Education for creativity

In the past, many people were educated to function in an industrial workplace. The needs of education today have shifted with the change to a post-modern, information-based, technological, globalised society. There is no longer a need for a multitude of 'worker bees'. Machines have made many jobs less labour-intensive, reducing the number of industrial jobs available. Different skills are needed to prepare people for employment, as redefined by technology.

During the modern era, it was believed that people could control the natural and social world. This 'certainty of modernity' is giving way to an understanding that nothing can be guaranteed – other than change and uncertainty. Change is inevitable and is happening more rapidly than ever before. The concept of a job for life, for instance, has become outdated, and few school, university or college leavers will be assured of salaried jobs.

The challenge for education is to prepare youth who are resourceful, imaginative and confident, who will find innovative solutions to the many challenges we face, and who are able to cope with change, with themselves and with one another. People will have to be able to visualise and make their own opportunities. The arts subjects are essential to prepare people for this purpose.

In South Africa, Creative Dance can play a vital role in bringing together a society torn apart by the violence and separatism of apartheid.

Children have grown up with race and class classifications imposed upon them. They have been culturally stereotyped in African, Afrikaner, Black, White and Coloured moulds. These stereotypes create barriers that prevent people from understanding one another, producing a prejudiced society. Through dance, children can learn more about themselves and, by understanding what motivates the self, begin to understand what motivates others. Because movement is common to all people, heedless of language and cultural barriers, and because dance is a communal activity, it is uniquely suited to social interaction and healing activities. Creative Dance activities can provide a vehicle for developing trust, enhancing inter-cultural understanding and celebrating both the uniqueness and the diversity of people.

Besides this capacity for social healing, dance has the potential to release tension that manifests itself as trappd energy in the body. Children growing up surrounded by violence become neurotic, tense and withdrawn. Research has highlighted the deep emotional tensions that work havoc when powerful feelings are checked within the mind, having no opportunity for expression. Tension or suppressed energy is often the trigger that leads to outbreaks of further violence. With interpersonal, family and township violence devastating our society, Shakti Gawain maintains that:

> if we are brought up in an environment that does not allow us to express a natural and creative kind of aggressive impulse, then it gets suppressed, only to come out later in a distorted and destructive form perhaps through violence towards others or towards ourselves or through emotional or physical ailments. (1989:75)

The same emotion understood, and with its energies transferred into another channel, becomes a source of personal power. Mental science is revealing more clearly the necessity for some form of creative art expression for a healthy mental life. Dance provides a creative outlet for anger. Energetic, physical activity that is also expressive can be a safe outlet for the tension created by strong emotions such as anger and hurt.

Dance as a vehicle for healing and transformation has special relevance in the attempt to bridge the gap between previously advantaged and disadvantaged pupils. This art form can provide a vibrant and enjoyable means of learning concepts across the curriculum. Its possible application in all subjects warrants exploration. It has the ability to revitalise and empower learners, encouraging them to participate in a way that differs from any other field of learning.

CHAPTER 2

Aims and outcomes

Previously, aims and objectives guided educators in identifying the content to be studied. 'Outcome-based education' is part of a new curriculum framework which makes education more accountable and assesses learners' knowledge and skills for qualification purposes. Teachers can no longer teach and hope that the pupils will learn. Pupils and teachers together must ensure that the outcomes are achieved.

General aims

Aims and objectives form the guiding principles for the design of outcomes. The general aims of teaching Creative Dance are to provide pupils with opportunities to:
• integrate physical (body), intellectual (mind), emotional (feelings) and spiritual aspects, to produce a well adjusted, balanced individual;
• develop the innate human potential for creative expression that is everybody's birthright;
• contribute to self-empowerment and social transformation.

In South Africa, Creative Dance could also contribute to:
• the healing and transformation of society;
• social and cultural reconstruction.

Without making unrealistic promises or claims, the following specific aims provide guidelines for teachers in their endeavour to lead pupils towards personal, social and cultural development.

Personal aims

To facilitate the development of the personality and innate potential of each individual, all aspects are important: the body, the mind, the soul and the feelings. These aspects are discussed separately, but in action the integration of these aspects is essential.

THE BODY

The body is the instrument of expression, the outer aspect of personality. A personality imprisoned in an unresponsive, stiff or painful body, lacks the advantage of a useful instrument.

To develop the body as an instrument and resource for communication and expression, pupils need to be guided to discover their *range of movement*, and assisted to extend this range through increasing *physical and motor skills* of co-ordination, balance, flexibility, stamina, mobility, control and strength.

Pupils need to learn how to care for the body to ensure its safety and on-going usefulness, to develop an understanding of *posture* and to use the body effectively and efficiently in action and stillness.

Body awareness – learning about personal space and general or shared space, learning to respect the working space of others – is important in the development of spatial orientation. With greater body awareness comes greater overall self-control, which is the first step towards self-discipline.

THE MIND

While Dance has been seen as primarily a physical activity for recreation and entertainment, its potential for developing the intellect is largely overlooked. One of the most urgent requirements of education in the 21st century is that it prepare and equip people

• for life and for living;
• for responding to and coping with change in an increasingly complex society;
• for being challenged by and learning from each experience;
• for being innovative, experimental, resourceful, self reliant, visionary and generative.

To release and foster creativity is one of education's greatest challenges. Dance, taught creatively, facilitates the development of imagination and creativity, lateral-thinking skills, problem-solving skills and decision-making abilities. In a country where pupils tend to be passive; promoting *critical thinking skills* is extremely important.

Dance is well suited for teaching values and learning concepts experientially from subjects across the curriculum (such as Maths, Science, Language, etc.) and for developing powers of focus and concentration which contribute to general learning ability. Dance can stimulate the mind to perceive, understand and remember and assist students to explore and experience, finding a balance between freedom and discipline.

Knowledge of dance terminology and vocabulary and an understanding of the underlying principles of movement are essential tools to enable learners to talk about, think about, write about and create dance.

THE FEELINGS

Art concerns creation. An artist creates by expression, transforming emotional experience through thought and intention into form. The audience/viewer completes the artistic creation by their feeling response. The real pleasure and value of a work of art, such as a painting, a dance or a symphony for the audience/viewer, is not so much in what we actually see or hear, as in how we react to what we perceive. An artistic creation that lacks an audience/viewer remains in the realm of self-expression.

By paying attention to and acknowledging the feelings felt and expressed through the body, we learn to deal with feelings appropriately. For instance, by providing an expressive, emotional outlet for tension and aggression through movement, in a safe environment, dance can contribute to a person's emotional health.

Through experiencing feelings of pleasure or satisfaction, and unconditional acceptance in a supportive atmosphere, a person gains confidence and develops his or her self-esteem. The aim would be to lose one's self-consciousness, to cultivate an attitude of tolerance and to become more understanding, sympathetic and respectful of the inner life of others, thus enriching one's own inner life.

Despite sweeping social and technological changes, humanity remains the same in its essential urges: to order, express and communicate an appreciation of truth and beauty as one sees it; to develop and reshape one's powers of expression into some new and better form; to enliven the intangible aspect of human personality, the spirit, to joy and self-fulfilment.

Social aims

Literature suggests a world-wide trend of alienation, isolation and fragmentation in peoples' lives. The healing qualities of touch and ritual, that are a feature of Creative Dance activities, assist individuals to rediscover trust and connectedness.

To integrate oneself within a group and co-operate intelligently with others, one must first feel the security and self-value which comes from integration with the self. Creative Dance provides a vehicle for learning to understand more about oneself. Self-understanding is required in order to understand others.

The healing of the individual has a ripple effect on the healing of society. Each person is part of the whole vast network of relationships and the more people change their consciousness and way of life the more the world changes. The more the world changes, the more individuals change. Dance can be an agent of change that cuts across class, race, gender and age to celebrate discovery, openness and interdependence.

Cultural aims

By reflecting and interpreting the ideas and values of the times, dance can contribute to building an inclusive South African culture. Derived from the diverse cultures, a cross-cultural approach should complement a poly-cultural approach. Insight into, and appreciation of one's own cultural heritage, recognising and analysing one's cultural values and assumptions, as well as those of others, contributes to a positive attitude towards the different cultures in our country. Albie Sachs said that instead of using culture as a weapon of struggle, as in South Africa's past, we should use culture in the process of transformation, to remove massive inequalities, to express our humanity in all its forms and to build a sense of pride, a self-affirmation (*1991: 187 – 193*).

Through Creative Dance, the learner should have the opportunity to:
• learn effective democratic practices of participation and negotiation without domination;
• develop abilities of leadership and followship, sharing, and a sense of responsibility and caring towards others;
• integrate oneself within a group and develop co-operative abilities as opposed to competitive learning;
• nurture an appreciation of the commonalities and diversity of people and become aware of the universality of dance;
• develop trust, sensitivity, awareness, self control, commitment and tolerance of others;
• learn through contact improvisation to rely on one another for physical support, to take responsibility for one's own and others' safety;
• cultivate the learning and understanding of non-verbal communication;
• develop abilities of self-evaluation and evaluation of peers within a constructive context.

Dance should be available for all who desire it. For the few who rise from the ranks to carry dance to its highest evolution, for the development of genius, there is a need for a sympathetic and understanding audience informed of the values and meaning of the art. An appreciation of the art of dance can be cultivated by providing opportunities to experience, see and read about it.

Specific Outcomes

While the syllabus guides a teacher in what material, concepts and processes need to be learnt, outcomes are the competencies that the learners have achieved and can demonstrate. The emphasis has shifted from a content-based education to an outcome-based education. Learners must be able to display certain competencies in progressive order at the various stages of their education. A competency is demonstrated by the ability to apply information and skills gained in a learning situation in order to complete a series of tasks successfully.

Specific Outcomes are the exact skills and information required in a particular situation. In order to ensure that education and training are taking place, an assessment of outcomes, based on performance criteria at each level, measure what a learner knows and can do. Such assessment also provides useful feedback, informs future practice, identifies needs and guides the learner. (See Chapter 5 on evaluation.)

Random examples of Specific Outcomes are listed below.

Students should show that they can:
• demonstrate an awareness of the body as a resource;
• understand the efficient, safe and healthy use of the body and mind;
• demonstrate fine and gross motor skills;
• demonstrate a balance between flexibility and strength;
• display co-ordination, control of body, flow of movement;
• remember, concentrate, take personal responsibility and practise self-discipline;
• demonstrate the ability to lead, follow, share and participate;
• demonstrate an ability to respond to and cope with change;
• display self-assurance, confidence and independence;
• display an ability to think laterally, make decisions, solve problems;
• work collaboratively towards common goals;
• show a degree of movement literacy in the ability to communicate through the use of non-verbal modes of expression;
• demonstrate the appropriate level of physical facility in the performance of floor work, centre work and moving through space;
• apply the principles of movements in dance;
• demonstrate in movement basic musical phrasings and rhythms;
• think imaginatively;
• organise ideas into movement phrases which can be manipulated to aid communication;
• be responsible and self-disciplined;
• utilise a range of techniques and styles to enhance performance quality;
• use dance terminology accurately in its application to set tasks and appreciation;

- understand and apply safe practices to exercise and dance;
- value their own and others' contributions in performance, composition and appreciation;
- understand how the development of dance has been affected by historical and socio-cultural patterns;
- demonstrate an understanding of the different South African cultural dance forms;
- recognise, analyse and display a sensory response to different dance styles, performances and functions;
- apply basic principles of dance analysis in critical appraisal;
- describe the functions of the arts;
- identify how the arts affect our lives;
- display knowledge of the necessary vocabulary to express an understanding of the elements and principles of dance;
- demonstrate an ability to create original material;
- demonstrate the ability to organise and create performances and exhibitions;
- demonstrate an understanding and awareness of principles of design;
- describe ways in which viewing, studying and creating dance may affect people.

SPECIFIC OUTCOMES FOR DANCE

GRADE 3	GRADE 6	GRADE 9
Be able to share space when performing actions	Use appropriate terms to describe and discuss aspects of Dance such as space, energy, levels, directions, rhythm	Demonstrate an awareness of aspects of space, shape and the environment and the body within it
Perform a range of simple actions such as running, stretching and balancing, with some control of body weight	Demonstrate movement co-ordination, flexibility, strength, mobility, control	Create and perform dances
Demonstrate an ability to concentrate	Recall and repeat with accuracy a series of actions	Show an ability to adapt quickly and effectively to swiftly changing situations
Be able to identify and perform basic locomotors and axial movements	Show control of direction, level and pathway	Demonstrate the ability to critically analyse dance performances
Demonstrate an awareness of the body	Be able to identify aspects of movement through the senses	Display an understanding of placement and healthy posture
Begin to identify good and bad body usage	Understand efficient, safe and healthy use of the body	Demonstrate an understanding of the care of the body as an instrument
Express and communicate ideas and feelings	Be able to express ideas, thoughts and feelings through dance	Explain how studying, creating and appreciating dance enriches peoples' lives
Demonstrate an ability to explore movement	Demonstrate a knowledge of movement principles	Use conventions of performance and presentation effectively
Talk about performances they have seen and identify what, who, how, why?	Demonstrate an ability to make decisions and choices, solve problems and think laterally	Draw on dance skills to demonstrate scientific or other cross-curricula concepts
Display an ability to share ideas and work co-operatively with a partner	Demonstrate an ability to share power, lead, follow and negotiate solutions	Show structured work devised with others
Be able to identify different dance forms	Demonstrate a knowledge of different kinds of dance and where they originated	Suggest factors that influenced the development of unique dance forms in diverse cultures
Remember and execute simple combinations of steps	Demonstrate an ability to be resourceful	Demonstrate an ability to organise and create performances
Display an ability to link actions together with increased fluency	Demonstrate an ability to create original material	Demonstrate a wide range of skills in creating, performing and appreciating dance
Be able to describe why they and other people dance	Demonstrate sensitivity towards others, the ability to work with others, express their views and listen to others	Experiment with fusion of dance forms and cultural forms
Learn a dance from a different culture	Identify possible occupations in Dance	Describe the different functions of the arts.
	Demonstrate an awareness of commonalities and differences in dance forms and competencies. Identify problems such as stereo-typing, prejudice	Explain how arts reflect the times we're living in
		Demonstrate an awareness of one's own and others' cultural assumptions

CHAPTER 3

Teaching method

The art of teaching Creative Dance will evolve differently for each person: what to teach and why, how to teach it, how to present it, when and for whom it is appropriate. These are some of the issues which each teacher resolves in his or her own way. However, knowledge gained from teaching experience and from the literature can provide insights to ease the journey of discovery.

Class structure and control

Before teaching Creative Movement to a new class it is essential to establish a class structure and control (see Chapter 6). Especially where classes are large, you will have chaos if controls have not been established. When there is chaos the children do not feel safe, do not enjoy themselves, cannot relax enough to really express themselves and may get hurt. It is unpleasant to teach and learn under such conditions.

A movement class is not a free-for-all. It involves a balance between giving and taking, concentrating and relaxing, being free and being restricted. Every teacher should work out their own balance of freedom and discipline. Obviously, authoritarian discipline is inappropriate to this kind of activity. However, setting clear expectations and ground rules enables learners to understand that self-discipline and a concern for others are pre-requisites for meaningful freedom and true self-expression.

Introduce and practise controls for the first few weeks with a new class. Even if it takes three weeks to establish control, it is not worth attempting anything else without it.

ESTABLISHING CONTROL

Run as fast as you can anywhere in the space ... freeze!

Bang the tambour or clap your hands and everyone immediately freezes. Practise this many times varying the locomotors (or types of movement) and adding changes of direction, level, shape and so on.

Jump up and down and make as much noise as you can! Freeze.

Lift your arm in the air and as your pupils begin to notice it, or one another, the silence creeps around the class. Practise this one over and over as well.

Run backwards – NO BUMPING. Anyone who bumps must sit down.

Ask the pupils why they should not bump into each other.

FREEZE GAME

Ask what something is like when it is frozen. Elicit that it cannot move.

Everyone hop, skip and jump and when you hear the beat of the tambour freeze immediately.

The last one to freeze is 'out' and anyone who moves at all, even blinking or giggling, is out. The last person 'in' is the winner.

Play this game a few times, varying the activities until the freeze is absolute and immediate.

Freeze

15

Try not to talk while the people are moving. Wait for absolute stillness and silence before you give the next instruction. This teaches respect: you wait for them to finish talking before you talk and they must do the same. If you talk while they move, some of them will not hear you. Then they will ask their friend what you said and the noise will continue or they will get frustrated because they will not know what to do. Explain the reason for rules, especially in South Africa where in the past so much teaching involved mindless discipline. Tell the students exactly how you will run the class and what you expect of them. Point out that there will be times for making noise and times for stillness' and that constant noise is very tiring.

Teacher attributes

The most competent teacher of Creative Dance is not necessarily a good dancer. Some of the least competent teachers are those who want to dance themselves and end up showing off to the students, or who push their own ideas rather than waiting for the children to develop their own.

The teacher must have enthusiasm for the subject. The teacher needs to be dynamic, and attract the students' interest; to be friendly, caring and interested; to have the perception to see what is happening; to be inventive and provide a wide variety of stimuli; to be encouraging and enjoy a sense of humour.

One of the most common errors is for teachers to talk too much. Lead the pupil to discovery and then stand aside and patiently wait for it to happen. Imposing solutions to problems or being too helpful can actually prevent the pupils from discovering their own resources and developing their problem-solving and negotiation abilities.

Teaching hints

• Alternate noisy energetic activities with soothing quiet ones.

• Use some kind of accompaniment to help structure the experience.

• Respond to the ideas and feelings of the class.

• Allow giggling or laughing. It is an expression of either enjoyment or embarrassment, or a release of tension. It is an emotional response – which is what this course is all about – providing an opportunity for self-expression.

• Make your instructions clear and brief. Do not give too many instructions at once. By your third instruction, they MAY have forgotten the first one.

• Create an atmosphere with your body, voice and music.

• Be well prepared, adaptable, interested and enthusiastic.

• Never stand in one spot to teach. Move amongst the students all the time and watch to see if they understand instructions or need encouragement.

• Plan the way to present Creative Dance for the first time, as this can affect the outcome of the whole programme and determine students' attitudes towards the subject.

• Start the class off with action rather than words to release tension, establish control and set the atmosphere. With children, begin with a large motor activity especially in winter when they need to warm up rapidly.

• Always finish the class on an encouraging, positive note.

• Always say 'Turn to the person closest to you', rather than 'Find a partner', to avoid rejection.

• Motivate through pleasure and accomplishment.

• Use your most important teaching tool, your voice, with variety: speak loudly and rapidly sometimes, and softly and slowly at other times.

• Reinforce the good and try to ignore mistakes. All feedback should be constructive, not destructive. Never make personal or sarcastic remarks.

• Touch is an important aspect of teaching dance. Always make sure that your touch is inoffensive, gentle and non-aggressive. If a child is being disruptive, stand next to him/her with your hand gently on his/her shoulder as you talk to the class. This usually works wonders in quietening and steadying the disruptive child.

• Enlist the co-operation of the class teacher so that dance has relevance within the school curriculum.

• Share the goal of the session with the class.

Potential problems

NON-PARTICIPATION

There are two schools of thought on the issue of non-participation. One view is that participation should be by choice; the other is that all pupils should participate. Be responsive to the situation. If pupils are self-conscious or unused to this form of dance, it is essential that everyone participate. This is more for the benefit of the whole class than for the individual. If some pupils are sitting out and watching, participants show off or become self-conscious and withdraw. Younger children accept a great deal without argument if it is presented as a matter of course. Older and adult pupils usually co-operate if the argument for participaton is explained to them. Initially at least we contend that participation should be non-negotiable.

TUNING OUT

Different pupils have different levels of involvement, as may the same child on different days. When a child is tuning out, encourage greater involvement by moving closer to the child. Alternatively, give the child attention in a non-threatening way. For example, move them to a different space or give attention to something they are doing as an inspiration for the next activity (Joe is lying on the floor with his elbows touching ... can you find a shape to make with your elbows?).

PRAISE AND BLAME

Never praise or blame individual performances; rather discuss the task. Ask 'did it work?' Emphasise the movement, not the child. If things do not go as expected, do not blame the children. It may be that the material or the situation is not suitable or the way it is being presented is inappropriate. Always look at yourself first before blaming the pupils. This does not mean that you cannot challenge the pupils to extend themselves. It is constructive and challenging to say something like 'that was really good, now let's see if you can jump higher' or 'use more energy' or 'vary your speed'. Rather than labelling children as problems, be sure that *you* are not inadvertently creating the problem. Sometimes problem pupils reflect problem teachers, uninteresting teaching, unsuitable material or a lack of structure.

DISCIPLINE

Never ridicule or threaten a child. Do not show one child up in front of others. Deal with individual discipline problems privately. It is distracting to interupt a class to scold someone. It breaks the atmosphere you have so carefully created and your own concentration. Avoid this by creating a strong structure and maintaining complete control.

Trouble can often be traced to one or two individuals with power over the rest of the group. Isolate them by quickly involving them. For example, 'Sandy bring the drum and when we're ready, begin to play a steady beat'. Children will only trust you if they know you can keep control of the group, and trust is essential for teaching successful creative movement.

EYES IN THE BACK OF YOUR HEAD

Beware of giving one child your full attention while the others get bored and stir up trouble. Treat the class as a whole. Learn to sense what is going on behind you, as you keep moving amongst the students and changing your position.

DISTRACTIONS

Other people passing or peeping can be very distracting; avoid having people watch until the class is really confident. They must join in or stay away.

INSTRUCTIONS

Use very few words. If you explain things over and over children will not bother to listen the first time.

If the students do not move, there is something wrong with the way you've set up the situation. Try rephrasing your instruction.

Be careful about demonstrating. Sometimes it helps to get them started, sometimes it distracts them. Never dance around as if it is your dance, not theirs. Pupils will either be de-motivated or will copy whatever you are doing.

APPROPRIATE MATERIAL

Be sensitive about your students' gender, age, cultural background and ability level.

Check that your material is appropriate for boys and girls, giving opportunities to move with strength as well as gentleness, fast as well as slowly, and making ugly and twisted as well as beautiful or curved shapes.

Children under eight years old may not be ready for group work. They are generally too individualistic at this age.

Be careful the imagery you use is appropriate for the age level especially when working with adolescents. Take an interest in what teenagers talk about and the kind of music they enjoy. Use these interests when planning the classes.

Between the ages of approximately 11 and 15, teenagers are very self-conscious about their bodies. Focus their attention on props, music, and concepts.

There will always be pupils of varying ability. Structure the class so that everyone has a sense of achievement and success whatever their level of expertise. Avoid comparing and discourage competing. Rather encourage a co-operative and collaborative attitude.

Be sensitive to different cultural norms. Try to make classes culturally flexible and provide opportunities for pupils to explore and discuss their own and others' cultural assumptions. Some people, for example, are comfortable with touching and eye contact and others are not.

Cultural background and age group affect attitudes towards touching and eye contact. There are times when contact improvisation may embarrass or be misused by pupils. Ensure an atmosphere of trust in the class (see Chapter 13) and set very definite rules of what is, or is not, permissible before embarking on touching activities. Avoid using touch exercises with adolescents or pupils who are very self-conscious.

Teaching very young children

Younger children between four and six years old are physically, emotionally and intellectually more vulnerable. Inappropriate handing at this age can actually be harmful and result in an adverse reaction to dance. While most of the practical activities suggested in this book can be adapted for young children, bear the following points in mind.

• Because their concentration span is limited, the class should not be longer than 30 to 45 minutes.

• Vary activities constantly. Look out for loss of concentration and be ready to change. Remember that small children both enjoy and feel secure with repetition. Therefore, even when introducing new activities, return to former ones constantly. Return to favourite activities if requested.

• In a creative atmosphere, discipline can be difficult. Falling around, unnecessary bumping, giggling and so on may indicate fatigue or a loss of concentration. At times like this change the activity or introduce a quiet time. For example, 'Lie down, close your eyes, and listen to the music.'

• Ritual is very important for small children (see Chapter 6). Always begin and end your class the same way. This helps children to focus and provides a familiar structure and sense of security.

• Children of this age are generally not ready for partnering or group work.

Music

Music can conjure up mental images and create atmosphere more quickly and easily than most stimuli. Collect all kinds of music, the more varied the better. You can use any kind of music from Classical to Percussion to Jazz, or home-made instruments and voice. Be wary of popular music, especially music with a very regular repetitive rhythm. Disco-type music can be limiting. Some pupils may become 'stuck' in the disco style and others may feel threatened and lose confidence.

Suitable clothing

Dress for comfort and freedom of movement. Bare feet are preferable so that the full range of foot movement is possible, and to prevent slipping or being stepped on by hard shoes. In winter, however, and on cold stone floors, allow pupils to wear soft shoes with rubber soles.

Teaching environment

If you have only a desk-crowded pre-fab classroom, get four strong students to push back the desks to leave the centre clear. If the space is very small, half the class can work while the others watch and participate by making appropriate rhythms or sound effects.

If you are next door to the library or other classrooms, try to reduce the noise level; a harsh incessant racket will make the movement class very unpopular with other teachers.

You may decide to work outside. Demarcate a specific and manageable area where all students are constantly in sight and are able to hear you easily.

CHAPTER 4

Lesson planning

In order to be free to create and to learn, learners need to be given a framework within which to work, with limits imposed by the teacher. Many teachers are not successful at teaching Creative Dance because they are not sure of their goals, or they confuse creativity with freedom. They may be wary of providing a structure for fear of being uncreative or too prescriptive. Very often they simply ask the class to move in any way they like to the music. This kind of 'total freedom' can be very threatening and lead to chaos or paralysis. Avoid asking students to dance freely with no guidance, directions or stimuli because students may run out of ideas and feel self-conscious.

Classes need to be carefully planned. Rather than compiling a list of unrelated activities, select and develop one idea/theme/principle so that students have a sense of completion at the end of the class. Choose material that is appropriate and of interest to the level, age and gender and culture of the class.

A structured lesson allows the class to concentrate on the instruction rather than focusing on themselves and getting self-conscious. Structure provides a clear starting point and allows the teacher to clarify the goal, present the lesson confidently and evaluate more easily. In fact, the more clearly the teacher has structured the lesson, the more confident he or she will be about allowing a different interpretation, or a change of direction from the class.

A lesson may consist of a number of overt and covert goals (see Chapter 2). However it is useful to select a specific goal for each class. This may be, for instance, to introduce one of the elements of dance. The teacher can, in this way, systematically cover the different elements and the contents of his/her syllabus. Students should emerge from a lesson with the sense of fulfilment that comes from having learnt something.

When preparing the lesson, keep in mind that words are very important. Think out instructions in advance. Avoid 'show me' which encourages exhibitionism. Rather use phrases such as 'see if you can ...' or 'experiment with ...'

Give enough detail for students to work from. Allow sufficient flexibility in the format of lesson plans for students to be able to contribute their own ideas. Lessons do not always go according to plan. Be ready to change the lesson plan if it is not working.

It may be helpful to follow an adaptable framework for lesson plans.

For example begin by answering these questions:
- What are the *aims and objectives* of the lesson? Where will my focus be?
- What are the expected *specific outcomes*? How will the learning activities achieve these outcomes?
- How will the session begin? Do I still need to practise controls, establish a trust atmosphere? How shall I introduce the *focus/theme*?
- What kind of *warm-up and skills training* will we need? How will it relate to the rest of the lesson?
- What kind of activities should I use for the initial *individual explorations?*
- How should these be *developed?* Would I include social interaction?
- What activity will give learners the opportunity to apply what they have learned during this process, interact socially and feel a sense of achievement.
- How will we discuss and *assess* what we have done? What questions can I pose to initiate discussion, to guide pupils to reflect critically on what they have done and to draw out or enhance understanding of the principles involved? How will I assess whether the learners have achieved the outcomes?
- What should we do at the end of the class to cool down, quieten and relax the students so that they are ready to proceed peacefully to the next class?
- What organisation is necessary for this class and what *equipment* will I need for the various stages of the lesson?

A suggested lesson plan could therefore be designed under some of the following headings:

> Aims and Objectives
>
> Intended Outcomes
>
> Introduction/Focus/Theme
>
> Warm-Up and Skills Training
>
> Individual Explorations
>
> Development and Social Interaction
>
> Assimilation or Application
>
> Discussion and Assessment
>
> Cool Down/Relaxation
>
> Organisation and Equipment

This is not a blueprint to be followed slavishly but a suggestion of one type of proven lesson plan.

A different approach is to structure a lesson plan into two parts:
• Part 1 is devoted to warm-up, movement education and exploration. This includes skills training and extension of movement vocabulary.
• Part 2 is aimed at application and apppraisal of content, plus the cool down.

All categories may not receive equal emphasis in each lesson and may even be omitted (depending on the lesson objective) and a variety of individual, partner or group situations may be used in part 1 or part 2.

We suggest that each lesson
• presents an element or focuses on a particular idea or theme
• links the skills training content with the rest of the lesson
• gives the pupils an opportunity for experimentation
• provides an opportunity to apply what they have learnt.

Written lesson plans

All teachers approach lesson planning differently, depending on training, school/college/university requirements, memory, confidence and experience. We recommend that you plan all your lessons in writing, in full, and build a file which will become an invaluable resource. This book was compiled from our combined lesson plans.

There are many different ways to prepare a written lesson plan. Each of the following sample lesson plans should take between 50 minutes and an hour, depending on the age group – the younger pupils are, the shorter their concentration span. Move the class to the next activity as soon as concentration wanes. This happens as they exhaust their own resources for a particular phase. On the other hand, if the class is still energetically inventing movement, try not to curtail it. If the lesson time is too short, then do part of the class next time rather than cut short enthusiastic and inventive work. It is still important to end the class with a sense of completion and accomplishment and begin the follow-up lesson with a recap.

Working with hoops

EXTENDING THE BODY POSSIBLITIES THROUGH THE USE OF PROPS

AGE: From 11 to adult   **TIME:** One to one-and-a-half hours

AIMS: To use props to stimulate movement invention.
To distract learners from limiting self-consciousness.

INTENDED OUTCOMES: The learners should demonstrate the ability to think imaginatively, participate actively, co-operate and display co-ordination and flow of movement.

INTRODUCTION AND WARM-UP: Place enough hoops well spaced on the floor to allow for one hoop per person.
Run very fast amongst the hoops without touching them. When the music stops freeze inside a hoop.
Remove a few hoops.
Run with hands clasped behind your back. When the music stops, release your hands and freeze surrounding the hoop. Run backwards amongst the hoops, again without touching them, and when the music stops freeze inside a hoop. If any part of you is outside the hoop you will have to sit out.
There will now be more than one person in some of the hoops.
Leap from hoop to hoop. Do not touch the floor other than inside the hoops. Freeze.
Play this game with many locomotor, level and direction variations, as long as the class remains interested.

SKILL TRAINING: Use the hoops in innovative ways during the skill training. Rolling down the spine combination
Swing combination
Knee alignment – gently bouncing knee bends, parallel and turned out
Feet articulation into jumps
Stretches

INDIVIDUAL EXPLORATION: Each person take a hoop and play with it. Use it as an extension of your body. See how many ways you can move with the hoop.

DEVELOPMENT: Find five different shapes using your body with your hoop. Join the five shapes together in a sequence. Pay special attention to the transitions from shape to shape.
Vary the timing, force, levels and directions (presuming they have explored these elements previously and are familiar with them).

APPLICATION AND SOCIAL INTERACTION: In groups of about five, using the hoops, 'democratically' create a theme dance for the Olympic Games.

DISCUSSION AND VALUATION: What did you notice about the use of symmetry and asymmetry?
Was there variation in speed, direction, levels? What did you find especially interesting about the different presentations?
What could have been done differently or changed and why?
What were the good experiences and bad experiences of working democratically?

AXIAL MOVEMENTS

AGE: From 8

AIMS: To draw attention to the many ways in which the body can interpret the same movement.
To promote flexibility and mobility; to encourage group co-operation and decision making.

INTENDED OUTCOMES: The learner demonstrates an ability to explore movement, perform a range of axial movements and link actions together.

EQUIPMENT: Large sheets of newsprint, one sheet for every six children plus an extra one, a drum, tambour or other percussive instrument or a simple percussive recorded rhythm. On each sheet of newsprint, except your own extra one, list, in large print

stretch   bend   swing   throw   twist   reach   collapse

INTRODUCTION OF THEME: Explore a number of simple everyday action sequences such as
- *stretch* up to a high shelf in the kitchen to take down a pot, and bend down to place it on the floor;
- *swing* a conductor's baton;
- *throw* a cricket ball to someone on the other side of the room;
- *twist* behind yourself to catch the ball;
- *reach* up on tiptoe to the very top of your cupboard to fetch a ball, lose your balance and
- *collapse* in a heap on the floor.

Identify the kinds of movements that these sequences involve. Do this by watching each other. Write down the movements as you identify them on your sheet of paper.

INDIVIDUAL EXPLORATION
As the teacher, beating on a percussive instrument to provide a rhythm, calls out the words, pupils explore each one. Focus on the meaning of these words. Experiment with as many different ways of expressing those words as possible.
Experiment with different versions of the same word by varying the texture of the sound you make, for example 'reeeach' (long and slow), 'reach' (short and sharp). In this way they will find many more ways of moving. Spend ten minutes on this and then another five minutes presenting the words in different sequences.

DEVELOPMENT AND SOCIAL INTERACTION
Divide the class into groups of six. If the class is small, use smaller groups but retain the six action words. Each group is provided with a sheet of paper on which the words are listed.
Work out a movement sequence using the words in the same order as listed. Pay attention to the following: relating to each other, making interesting patterns and using the words inventively. Finally, each group performs their sequence for the others.
In the last process, at least twelve to fifteen minutes should be allowed for the groups to interact, plan, try out and practise their sequence. A further fifteen minutes is needed for each group to perform their sequence, repeating it at least twice. A percussive instrument can be used to accompany the sequence, allowing one sound per movement or with older students allowing them to find their own rhythmic phrase by using a simple recorded percussive rhythm.

DISCUSSION AND EVALUATION
Discuss (valuact) the different presentations, drawing attention to how differently each group used the element and how much variation in movement we are capable of.

Possible progressions from the previous lesson

You do not have to do something completely new each lesson. Small children enjoy repeating activities and, second or third time around, they are far more confident. Sample lesson 2 (Axial movements) can be:

- Repeated as is with very small children.
- Repeated using different words – sway, shake, and so on.
- Repeated using different groupings of the words. For example, return the sheets of paper to the same groups. With younger children use the back of the sheet to list the words in a different order. With older students, allow them to list the words as they choose. Each group then presented the sequence and the class guess the order of the sequence.
- Repeat as above, but with each person in the group following a different sequence so that a really interesting movement phrase is created.
- Create a class movement sequence by joining together all groups' phrases, and adding a musical accompaniment.

CHAPTER 5

Assessment and evaluation

The impulse towards creativity must be nurtured in a special way. Psychological safety evolves from an emphasis on acceptance and understanding of the individual (*Hawkins, 1964*). In a movement class, the student needs to feel accepted by the teacher as an individual of unconditional worth and creative ability. Preconceived standards and competition should be de-emphasised to free students to work creatively. There needs to be an understanding that all creative effort will be respected even when the results do not reach the desired goal. Pupils need to be reassured about those aspects of their work that are successful. This kind of learning climate fosters creativity and through sharing and performing their work, students overcome feelings of isolation and increase their sense of belonging.

Grading dance achievement, therefore, can be frustrating because it seems to contradict this philosophy. However, if a subject is not assessed, pupils do not receive feedback about their progress. Furthermore, in our current education system, children learn from an early age to be extrinsically motivated, to work for rewards such as marks or grades, so if they are not evaluated in dance, they begin to judge the subject as less important.

Learning, teaching and assessment are inextricably linked in outcome-based education. Assessment has a developmental and monitoring function to fullfil, to determine whether or not outcomes have been attained, as a means to assist teaching and learning. Assessment relates to the process of obtaining information which allows teachers, pupils and parents to make judgements about a learner's progress. The essence of assessment is determining what the learner is actually achieving in relation to expectations of attainment and drawing conclusions from that comparison. (*Western Cape Education Department, 1996*).

Assessment may be:

• *Summative*: A summary of what has been achieved at the end of a unit of teaching and learning
• *Formative:* Information about the student which may be helpful in assisting further development
• *Norm-referenced assessment*: An approach designed to make comparisons with other learners in the class
• *Criterion-referenced assessment:* An approach in which grades are given according to a predetermined level of competence.
These aspects combine to form the elements of a coherent system for the holistic assessment of learners.

FORMAL SUMMATIVE ASSESSMENT

This includes the award of yearmarks, credits and qualifications, and recording and reporting these. The assessment may be internally or externally moderated.

ON-GOING FORMAL CONTINUOUS ASSESSMENT

Continuous assessment should be an integral part of teaching and learning. A learner's achievements should preferably be assessed relative to his or her personal abilities (criterion-referenced) rather than compared to the achievements of other learners (norm-referenced). In order to identify the learner's strengths, weaknesses and needs, continuous assessment should establish:

• what learners know
• what learners understand
• how well learners communicate what they know and understand
• what learners can do
• how well they do it.

Continuous assessment should enable educators and learners to reflect continuously on their work, and guide the teacher to plan the next step.

Day-to-day assessment can be handled as part of the teaching process through 'valuaction', a term coined by Halprin (*1974*) to cover evaluation, feedback and decision-making with an emphasis on action. Valuaction sessions encourage the discussion of alternatives, comments and critiques. These discussions provide the opportunity for pupils to make sense of what they are doing and learning, to make and hear constructive suggestions and to get feedback on their progress.

Criterion-referenced assessment

Assessment is usually made in relation to set criteria or 'unit standards' of achievement. A learner's progress is measured against criteria that indicate attainment of learning outcomes, rather than against other learners' performances.

It is worthwhile to involve older students in identifying and discussing the criteria to be used. Especially if a numerical grade rather than a comment is required, the teacher should ensure that the pupils understand the criteria for grading them.

Some of the aspects in creative movement that can be assessed are:
• personal skills such as confidence, creativity, application to tasks, technical capability
• cognitive skills such as thinking, experimenting, understanding
• social skills such as the ability to work together, communication, empathising, leadership.

Criteria to evaluate a pupil's work and identify specific outcomes include:
• Is the intention of the dance clearly communicated? How?
• Is the movement inventive? In what way?
• Does the work demonstrate an understanding of the elements? concentration? self-discipline? responsibility? participation? co-operation?

Assessment criteria should be drawn from expected outcomes (see Chapter 2).

Self-assessment by the teacher

After a class, evaluate how it was presented, identify mistakes and learn from them, and try not to blame the students if things went wrong.

Useful questions for self-assessment include:
- How appropriate is the work for the learners' abilities and stages of development?
- How aware are the learners of what is expected? How do I know this?
- Is the work being conducted at an appropriate pace?
- Are learners enjoying the work? How do I know?
- What particular learning needs are being revealed?
- To what extent are learners taking responsibility for learning?
- What factors interfere with learning?
- Are any learners out of place or isolated in the classroom? What can I do about them?
- Is my teaching adequate, challenging and inspirational?

It should be noted that all the following sections are interrelated and although the concepts are dealt with separately, a combination of elements is inevitable and is to be encouraged.

PART TWO

Theory into Practice

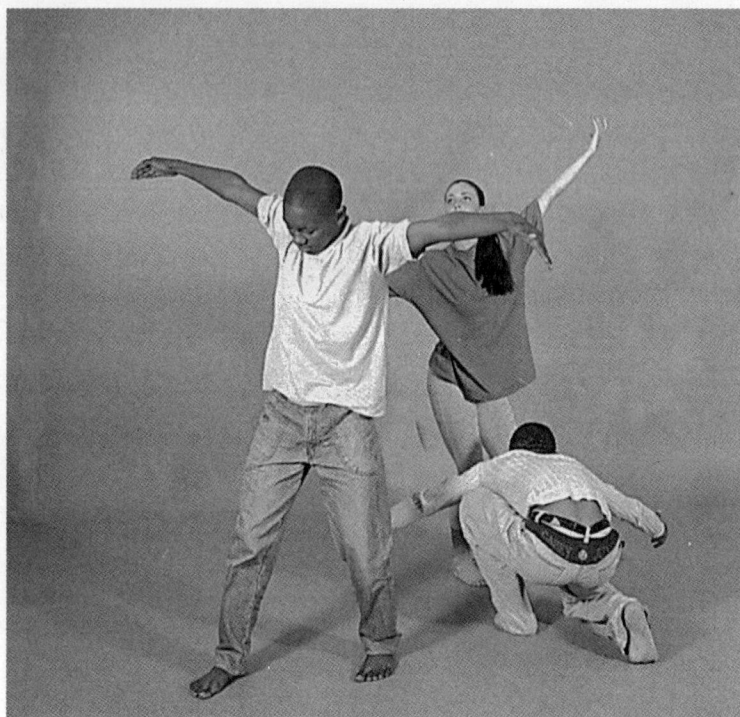

CHAPTER 6

Warm-up and skill training

'The way in which you present movement for the
first time can affect the outcome of the whole programme'
(Nicholls)

There are various ways to begin a dance programme. Some educators prefer to explain briefly to the students what to expect. Our experience from 25 years of teaching has been that learners need to be 'thrown in at the deep end'. They should have a safe, busy, fast, non-threatening, fun-filled experience with a lot of laughter and release opportunities, culminating in a discussion at the end of the session. Learners should not have time to become self-conscious. If their first experience is a positive one, the dance programme has a chance of success.

It is vital to create a structure in the class, especially when teaching a subject that encourages freedom of expression (see Chapter 3). This structure provides a framework for the educator and for the learners; it helps the educator to plan the lesson; it gives the learners a sense of security within a situation that is in other ways free of boundaries and full of the unexpected. People cannot feel free to participate fully unless their physical and emotional safety is assured. There cannot be freedom without discipline. Creative effort is nurtured best in an atmosphere that is permissive, but permissiveness does not imply a lack of structure.

One way of establishing a structure in the class is to evolve a *ritual*, a pattern of operation, which pupils begin to recognise and which can give them a sense of security as to what to expect and what is expected of them. This can be achieved through a fairly predictable ritualistic warm-up followed by, and complementing, an unpredictable creative section. Learners learn, then, to expect the creative class to unfold in this way. Skill training requires a certain amount of repetition and therefore this section of the class provides an opportunity for establishing a ritual-like pattern.

Some of the following could be incorporated within the warm-up and skill training ritual:
• an exercise to focus the attention on the body, the dance and the moment, developing powers of concentration
• 'controls' practice
• an exercise to release pent-up tension
• an exercise to establish an atmosphere of trust
• warming up the muscles and increasing the breathing, preparing the body for action
• skill training exercises.

Ritual

A ritual is a pattern or a recognised procedure, repeated on a regular basis which is relatively predictable. We all engage in certain rituals on a daily basis, whether it is brushing our teeth, exercising or following the same route to work or school. These routine activities are comforting in their predictability. A warming-up ritual has the same effect. It provides an opportunity for repetition which is important for building technique, concentration, stamina and control; and is comforting in a class which emphasises experimentation and exploration of the unknown. The younger the student, the more need there is for a strongly structured warm-up ritual.

Focus

On entering the dance space there is usually a need to bring one's thoughts to focus on Dance, away from the distractions of previous and future activities, thoughts and problems. Focus or concentration, like any other skill, needs to be practised and will have positive repercussions in all aspects of one's life.

Controls

Until controls are firmly established, the practice of controls cannot be over-emphasised. Establishing what is acceptable and what is not, is essential for students to feel safe, to participate in negotiating the controlling mechanisms and to develop self-discipline. There is a need for very few rules. For example:
• no bumping – discuss with students why it is important for everyone to be responsible for their own and everyone else's safety
• freeze on the loud bang of the drum
• freeze when the teacher raises her hand in the air (or some pre-arranged gesture). The freeze rules must be consistently used. They cannot be negotiable or the class control will disintegrate. Only give instructions when the class is completely 'frozen' (see Chapter 3).

You may need to set *spatial boundaries* especially if working outside or in a large hall. (Small children can be overwhelmed in a large space, so demarcate part of a hall for use.) Students may have to be told to keep off certain objects, furniture or equipment. Set the boundaries early on in the lesson.

Running and freezing

Release

Trapped energy stored in the body as tension may exist in students as a result of frightening experiences, difficulties in the classroom, in the home or in the community. Sitting for long hours in a classroom is not natural and many children have a need to release pent-up energy when they arrive in a hall or outdoor space. This tension could ultimately lead to uncontrolled or anti-social behaviour or, even disease if it is not provided with a natural outlet. The Creative Dance class is an ideal opportunity to release tension in a controlled and protected environment.

Trust

Learning to trust, first oneself and then one another, is essential for establishing a frame of mind that is open to learning, exploring and developing good social habits. Apart from being necessary to promote creativity, it is one of the aspects of dance education that can be transformative, that can contribute to an improvement in social relationships. An atmosphere of safety and acceptance needs to be created in the classroom for trust exercises to be successful. Situations that create feelings of insecurity and self-consciousness and destructive practices such as sarcasm and ridicule must be avoided. Trust develops over time and therefore trust exercises should be an on-going part of the ritual. (For trust exercises, see Chapter 14.)

Warming up

A warm-up may begin with breathing exercises or exercises such as swings that increase the breath intake. Oxygen creates energy so increasing intake at the beginning of a class gets sluggish students going. To avoid injury, muscles need to be warmed up. Warm up each part of the body and pay attention to principles

Stretching the whole body to warm up

Correct spinal alignment

of good body use, especially of the vulnerable neck and spine. Whether you use a particular technique of dance warm-up or a more general aerobic warm-up, watch the class carefully and give specific instructions and corrections where necessary. Avoid turning your back on the class and 'performing' a warm-up while the students copy. Ultimately you are responsible for the safety of the students and must keep a vigilant watch for movement habits that may cause injury.

The warm-up may be a series of formal, taught exercises or it may be more informal using open-ended creative directions such as locomotor movements. Gradually build up a ritualised warm-up sequence and repeat it at the beginning of each lesson. A regular warm-up affords an opportunity to enlarge the learner's movement vocabulary, develop movement memory and learn skills.

Skill training

Skill training here includes general physical proficiency as well as specific dance abilities or techniques. In dance, the body is the instrument, and movement is the medium. The mind needs to be trained to use the body and the body must be trained to be responsive to the mind.

There is a conflict inherent in combining technical skill training – which has a right or wrong aspect – with creative objecives – where there is no right and wrong and whatever the person creates is an expression of their uniqueness. Pupils need to be made aware of and understand this contradiction.

In a Creative Dance class, learners need to develop strength, flexibility and co-ordination, and thus become more responsive, articulate and sensitised as the range of their body's capabilities is extended. In all dance training, however, technique is a means to an end rather than an end in itself.

Creative movement classes that do not provide skill training quickly become boring as students reach the limits of their natural movement abilities. Unless there is a growth in strength, flexibility and command of the body, the sense of fulfilment from Creative Dance will be short-lived and incomplete. As students become more proficient in creative movement, they will find they need greater technical skill in order to fully express their ideas. The goal of technique is to allow one to move safely and efficiently.

The approach to skill training should not be authoritarian. Encourage learners to be aware of correct technique and to understand why one way of doing something is preferable to another.

A way to work technique-building into a creative class is to begin with one skill-building exercise and at each subsequent session, repeat the exercise(s) previously learnt and add a new one.

Skill training will vary from teacher to teacher. There are, however, some skills that are universal, to ensure movement quality and flow, and the safe use of the body:
• An awareness of the correct use of the neck and spine, for example learning to sit with the spine straight (no slouching) and to stand in correct postural alignment (not slouching or over-arching); learning not to squeeze the neck (not dropping the head backwards on the neck or scrunching the neck as in head circling exercises), to protect the nerves that run through the spinal cord in the neck from the brain to the body;
• Clarity of, and quality in, actions for example exension of the feet and legs in jumping, for elevation;
• Extension of movements beyond ordinary, everyday actions, to enhance flow of movement and movement quality;
• Safety when landing from jumps or leaps. The toes touch the floor first, followed by the heels and the bending of the knees. One should never land flat-footed; it is too much of a shock for the spine, knees and ankles;
• The correct alignment of the knees over the middle toes when bending or landing, to avoid twisting the knees and causing debilitating injuries:

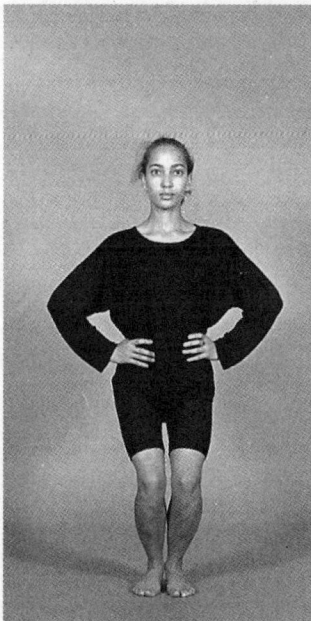

Prepare

Jump

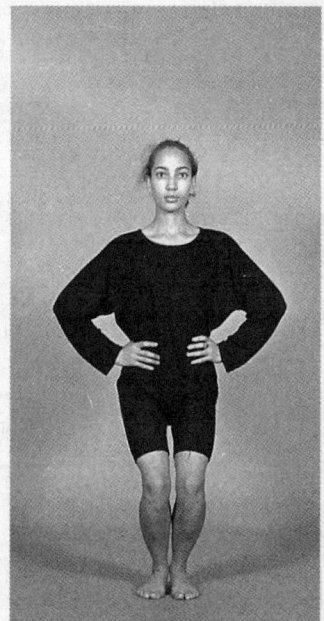

Land

• An understanding of the principle of balance;
• Control of the body moving in the space provided;
• Increase of mobility and flexibility;
• Building of stamina and strength so that the body is supported in the dance activities;
• Awareness of the ebb and flow of movement through breath;
• Awareness of the fall and recovery of movement, the use of weight;
• Moving from the centre of the body for powerful expression and to develop movement flow.

Demand and expect improved performance at every session. Sloppy work should not be accepted. Skill training helps develop a language or vocabulary of movement that will facilitate expression. Technique needs to become internalised through practice and repetition so that dancers do not have to concentrate on technique but can give their whole attention to expression and communication.

Getting started

When beginning creative dance with a new group, use a name game or an ice breaker to relax learners and to get them going.

NAME GAME 1 (ICE-BREAKER)

Students stand in a circle.
Each person takes a turn at sounding out their name and finding a simple movement pattern which expresses the name. For example, the name Steven is sounded out as Steeeeee vin with a long stretching movement followed by a short, staccato one. Everyone repeats the name and movement of each person.
New names are learnt very quickly especially if you go round the circle a number of times increasing the speed of presentation.

NAME GAME 2 WITH BALL (ICE-BREAKER)

Stand in a circle. Say someone's name and then throw them the ball. Keep this up getting faster and faster until everyone knows the names of the whole group·

NAME GAME 3 WITH LOCOMOTORS (ICE-BREAKER, WARM-UP)

Run anywhere in the space … freeze. Introduce yourself to everyone around you. Skip fast about the space … freeze. Introduce yourself to everyone near you. See how many names you remember.
Repeat this game with many varied locomotors until people know one another's names.

LOCOMOTOR WARM-UP EXERCISES

Simple running or other locomotor activities provide an opportunity for establishing controls and releasing energy. Energetic activity accompanied by a percussive instrument is recommended. Vary the format by using skipping or other locomotors. There is no limit to the possible variations.

LOCOMOTOR – FREEZE (RELEASE, CONTROLS, WARM-UP)

Run fast and stop suddenly, freeze.
Run backwards with no bumping, freeze.
Run sidewards and touch all four walls.
Run with knees high and freeze low.
Skip backwards while shaking hands, freeze in a twisted shape.
Gallop forwards while clapping hands, freeze in a soft round statue.
Run with a partner and freeze to form a picture.
Run in unison using increasingly larger groups.

BALLOON OR BAG (BREATHING, FOCUS)

Imagine that you are a crumpled plastic bag (or balloon). Someone begins to blow air in to you and you get bigger and bigger and bigger until you pop!

FOCUS (ICE-BREAKER, RELEASE)

Pat your face gently with your finger tips. Pat the top of your head and down your neck, across your chest (gently), hard across your stomach, down your legs, up the back of your legs, getting harder and harder across your buttocks. Stand very still and focus on a spot somewhere in the room. Don't let anything or anyone distract you. Don't let your eyes wander. Don't let your mind wander. Be in control of your mind. On the beat of the drum instantly find a new focus spot.
Repeat a few times.
Focus on a spot on someone's body. Change your level or direction and find a new focus spot on someone else's body. Now slowly and smoothly without taking your eyes off that spot, move towards your spot.
This usually ends in laughter as students all follow their moving spots.

SIMON SAYS (FOCUS)

Play a game to increase movement vocabulary and develop concentration. When a command is proceeded by 'Simon says' carry it out, but when the command is not proceeded by 'Simon says', do not do it. If you do, you are out. For example,
Simon says lift your arms. Simon says kick your leg. Clap your hands.
(If you clapped your hands you are out!)

SWINGS

Swinging warms up the whole body simultaneously, needs little effort and teaches co-ordination.
Put together swinging combinations
These may be very simple at first and then develop in complexity. Teach one combination for a few weeks, until the pupils are comfortable with it, before moving on to a variation. Direction and pathway may be added as progressions. Once the students know the exercise let them dance it facing another person. Each time they complete the sequence, give four counts for them to run spontaneously to a new place in the room and face whoever is closest before dancing the sequence again.

COOL DOWN AND STRETCHING

At the end of each class provide an opportunity for cooling down, quietening down and relaxing. This is also the best time to stretch as the muscles are warm and pliable.

Stretching exercises should take place on the floor rather than standing so that the body is supported. Balance the stretching and strengthening of muscles so that students do not become weakened with over-stretching or muscle-bound with over-strengthening. Avoid bounces while stretching as they cause wear and tear on the ligaments. Young children stretch easily but the concentration at this level should be on general lengthening of the whole body and the limbs, rather than specific muscle groups.

**Hip flexors
stretch**

**Hamstring
stretch**

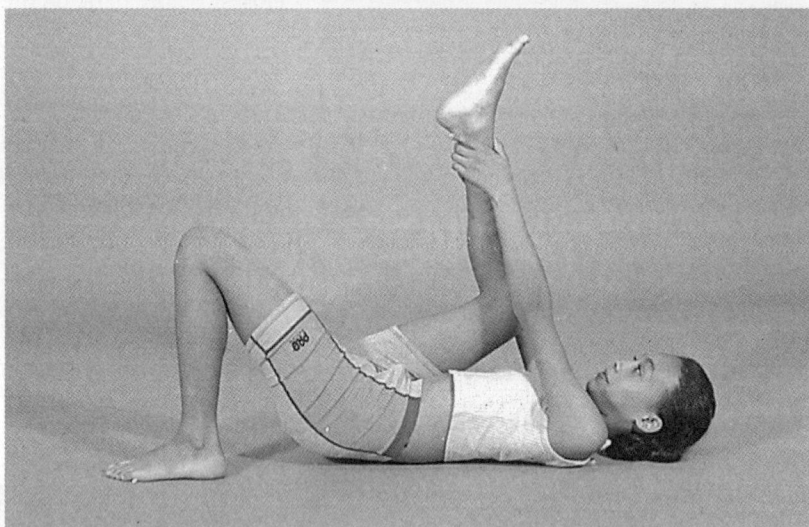

**Quadriceps
(thigh muscle)
stretch**

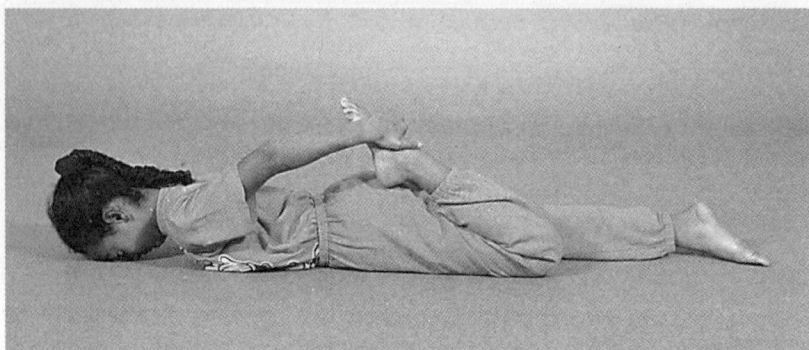

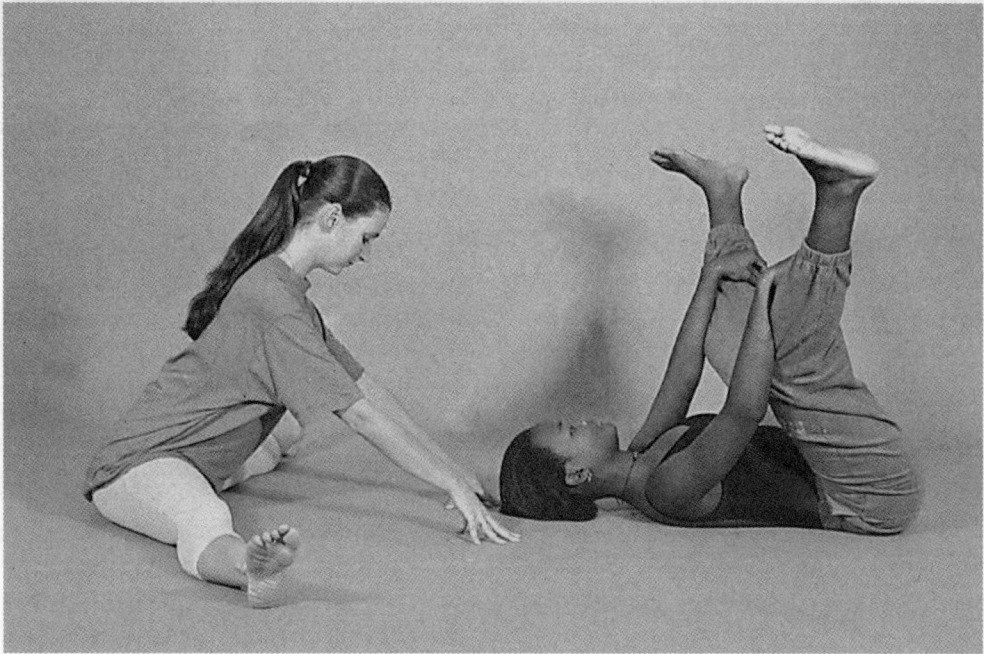

Adductors (inner thigh) stretch

Lateral (side) stretch

TRUST EXERCISE

Walk anywhere in the space in time to the drum beat. Ignore everyone and just walk.

Keep walking but begin to acknowledge one another in any way, with a nod, a smile, a wink. If you want to, join or follow someone as you walk, then leave them and join someone else.

Think about whether you are the kind of person who is outgoing, who looks for others to join or whether you are more introvert, waiting for people to come to you. When someone joins you … does it feel as if your personal space is being invaded or are they welcome? How does it feel when they leave? Do you feel a little rejected?

Continue with the above but add instructions to lean forwards, backwards or sideways. Lean softly against the furniture or walls. Keep walking and leaning, but also add leaning against another person. Make sure you make eye contact with that person before you lean, otherwise they may not expect you and may drop you.

Make sure no-one is dropped – this is a trust exercise so be responsible for one another. When someone leans against you, gently lower them to the floor. When you lean against someone, give them your weight and soften your body. The very adventurous may try jumping into someone's arms.

In small groups discuss the concept of trust and your response to this type of physical contact.

(For more trust exercises, see Chapter 13.)

Outcomes

These are some of the outcomes to be achieved in skill training. Students should show that they can
• demonstrate the appropriate level of physical facility in the performance of floor work, centre work and moving through space
• understand the efficient, safe and healthy use of the body and mind
• demonstrate fine and gross motor skills
• demonstrate a balance between flexibility and strength
• display co-ordination, control of body, flow of movement
• remember, concentrate, take personal responsibility and practise self-discipline.

CHAPTER 7

The body as instrument

No two bodies are alike and no two people express themselves in exactly the same way. We speak of the body as an instrument of expression, but it is more like a whole orchestra. Each separate part has its own quality of movement.

EXPLORE BODY PARTS WITH IMAGERY

Fingers – play an imaginary piano, walk through the yellow pages; climb the stairs; perform a thumb duet; click, tap, point, clench, circle, scratch, stroke, tickle ...

Hands – clap a tune; rub; smack, press a sticky toffee and then try to pull your hands apart; your hands are twitching and you can't stop them; wash your hands; open and close, squeeze a wet sponge ...

Make up a chant or song with body words and movements, for example 'Knees and toes, knees and toes, head and shoulders, knees and toes.'

EXPLORE SEPARATE BODY PARTS WITHOUT IMAGERY

Sit on the floor in a comfortable position. Close your eyes. Begin to move your head, any way at all. See how many different ways you can move it, turn it, drop it, shake it, forwards and backwards. When you find an interesting movement develop it, repeat it, vary it. Let the upper spine be drawn into the movement and then the whole body.

Repeat with shoulders, elbows (emphasise the angularity), wrists, fingers, the whole hand, the whole arm, the trunk.

Lying down, try to move your hips in different ways. You don't have to remain on your back. Lifting your legs in the air, see how you can move your knees, ankles, toes, whole leg, whole body.

Experiment with your face. Make faces: stretch it, twist it, make it wide, narrow, long, short.

COMBINATIONS OF PARTS

Move hands and feet in relation to one another. Create an elbows and knees dance, an arms and legs dance, or a trunk and head dance.

CONNECTING PARTS

Attach one part of the body to another, for example elbow to knee. See what you can do despite the restriction. Connect any two different body parts and, maintaining the shape, find a way to travel.

HEAD DUET

Find an interesting position to begin your study – stand, sit or lie back to back, facing one another or side by side, far apart or close together. Begin with a moment of quiet, and then begin to move your head any way you wish. Work co-operatively, create the movements together and allow the dance to reach its own natural conclusion. Pause for a moment in your last position before breaking your concentration and coming out of your dance. Discuss with your partner what seemed to work and what did not work.

Try the same with different body parts and varying numbers in the group, for example an arms trio, a legs quartet.

CHALLENGES THROUGH RESTRICTIONS

Restricting movement can stretch the imagination and generate new ways of moving.

Place one arm behind your back and move freely. See how your movement is affected and how you compensate. Now put both arms behind your back. Then use both arms freely but tuck one leg up.

RESTRICTIONS 2

Use restrictions to devise new kinds of animals. For example, keep two arms behind your back and become a crawling animal. Join with another person who has tucked one leg away and form an entirely new creature. Give your creature a name and a sound.

LEADING, FOLLOWING, SENDING, GOING AWAY, GOING AROUND, AVOIDING, STRIKING

Explore leading with your shoulder, hips, belly button.
Follow your nose, fingers, ear.
Send your head, arm, hand.
In pairs send one another, carefully.
Do not 'send' roughly or into a wall.
Experiment with any body parts – going away from, avoiding and going around one another.
Experiment with body parts striking one another in such a way as to cause a sound. With a partner, explore movements and sounds caused by touch.

SPINAL RUN

Run while moving the spine through a variety of positions, for example run with a round back, run with a flat back, run while twisting to look behind you. Feel the movement in the spine. Take the movement beyond plan or habit – do not plan what you are going to do, be spontaneous and challenge yourself to do something you've never done before.

FOCUS ON BODY PARTS

Focusing on your hand, move it slowly and smoothly over your head, around your body, behind you. Gradually allow your focus to shift to your hip; move it in as many ways as you can. Allow other parts to join in but let the hip be the leader.
Allow the focus to change again to another body part, and continue.

'Sending' the head

CIRCLES

Make little circles in the air with one finger or with your nose. Make larger circles with your wrists, elbows, knees and feet. Make gigantic circles with your arms, legs and whole body. Make circles going in different directions with each shoulder. Make circles with elbows and knees at the same time. In pairs and larger groups circle around one another using different parts of the body.

FIGURE 8s

Draw figure 8s in the air with your hands, ankles, knees and elbows. Using any part of the body let one figure 8 lead to another. Compose a figure 8 solo dance using different body parts, and varying the size and velocity of the movements.

CONVERSATIONS

Have conversations with different body parts. Let the one hand make a movement which is answered by the other hand. Try this with unusual combinations of body parts, for example, the torso 'speaks' to the feet.
Try this in pairs. As in verbal conversations ensure that one body 'speaks' while the other 'listens'.

PALM TOUCH

Turn to the person closest to you. Stand facing one another. Decide who will lead first. The leader places his/her hands up front as if on a mirror. The partner places his/her hands on the leader's hands. The leader briskly and sharply keeps changing the position of his/her hands while the partner constantly tries to keep the hands in contact.
After a few minutes, change over leadership.

Movement characteristics of body parts

Some movements are characteristic of a
particular body part. For instance, you
can smile with your face or you can allow
that smile to be expressed with your
whole body. The following table contains
words that one usually associates with a
particular body part.

The multiplier effect of multiple bodies

Exploring the movement possibilities of
your own body can be extended to
exploring the possibilities generatd by
using connected bodies. The range of
movement possibilities becomes far richer
and infinitely more exciting to perform
and to watch. Furthermore, physical
contact can be a powerful means of
liberating individuals from the confines of
their own separate personalities, building
trust and shifting attention to the multiple
possibilities inherent in a group, however
small or large.

Express the unique quality of these words using the whole body. Exaggerate!

FACE	HANDS	ARMS	LEGS
smile	open	punch	kick
frown	close	strike	shuffle
sneer	clench	grind	stamp
pout	grab	sweep	trample
scowl	stroke	cut	tip-toe
grin	scratch	slice	scuff
yawn	squeeze	chop	slip
chew	wring	push	creep
grimace	knead	pull	stumble
blink	snatch	thrust	tap
glare	slap	dig	drag

JOINING BODIES

Holding hands is a universal means of establishing contact and can break down any initial reserve about touching or being touched.

In twos, holding right (or left) hands together, see what movements you can make.

Try holding your partner's opposite hand: A's left hand holds B's right hand. See how that affects your movement.

Try this with three people or keeping contact with only the tip of one finger. Explore variations using different body parts and different size groups.

Try heads touching, feet touching, backs touching, palms together, hands on one another's hips, elbows touching, and so on.

PASSING THE WEIGHT

Give your weight to your partner – lean against your partner – and give your partner support.

Find many ways to pass the weight back and forth. Choose four or five ways and develop the transitions between each position.

For older learners and after trust has been established, add the challenge of lifting one another off the ground completely.

Lifting and supporting your partner

CHAPTER 8

The body in action

All movements occur through space *(locomotor)* or around the spine *(axial)* or combine both aspects. Locomotor movements travel from place to place – they go somewhere. Axial movements move around or along the axis of the body, which is the spine. Most movements combine these two aspects, for example walking is a locomotor that moves across space with an axial oppositional spiral movement of the upper torso.

Locomotor movements

According to Rudolf Laban's analysis of movement, there are eight basic locomotor movements and all other locomotor movements are modifications of these:
walk   run   leap   hop
jump   skip   gallop   slide
As a means of broadening one's movement vocabulary, locomotor movements should initially be explored separately, encouraging travelling and a freedom of movement, and accompanied by simple rhythms or music.

WALKING EXPLORATIONS

Walk anywhere in the room in time to the beat.
Leader beats the tambour, drum or any percussive instrument or uses music with a walking rhythm.
Walk tall ... walk low to the ground ... walk in a zigzag, use your arms in an unusual way ... walk as if you are exhausted ... excited ... miserable ... petrified ... apprehensive ... outraged. Walk very fast ... very slow ... with a limp ... in the army ... wounded ... stalking ... on tiptoe ... through mud in your grandfather's gumboots ... on thin ice over a freezing lake ... over hot coals from a fire ... through long grass. Create an outrageously silly walk ... walk in an interesting rhythm and add a turn.
The variations are endless.

WALKING DANCE

Choose four walks that you like and string them together to make a movement sentence – a walking dance. Turn to the person closest to you and teach one another your walking dances. Arrange whether you are going to do them simultaneously, facing one another, back to back, side by side, or in opposite directions. Make sure you have a starting and

Walking explorations

ending position. Add variations in direction, level and speed. Add moments of stillness.
Allow half the class to watch while the other half performs and vice versa.

RUNNING EXPLORATION

Run anywhere in the space as fast as you can. Whenever you meet another person, wall or object make a sharp turn and keep running. Emphasise NO BUMPING.

Run backwards, sidewards, add sudden stops and freezes in a statue. For example, run low, freeze in a low statue, run as if on hot coals, freeze in a high position, and so on.

Other running ideas are:
• run as if being chased;
• run as if on a fragile frozen lake;
• run in slow motion;
• run and stop suddenly;run in twos holding hands and keeping pace with one another
• run as if wearing gumboots in mud; run as if to catch the bus;
• run as if in a movie that is on fast rewind;
• run and stop gradually;
• run in a large group, keeping pace.

RUNNING DANCE

Compose a running dance. Use at least three different runs and create an interesting floor pattern. Vary the directions. Add stops.

Work out a group running dance using only running steps, stops, direction and level changes, and a variation in focus.

53

GOING AND STOPPING

Start by developing a feeling for stopping and starting.

Improvise with the words stop, start, freeze, go, hold, continue, wait and arrive. Then form and perform your own list of 'stopping and starting' words.

Focus on the contribution which each body part gives to the action, for example elbow, fingers and feet leading, chest rising, hips twisting. Emphasise the contrasts, such as suddenly freezing or slowly settling; hovering high or collapsing low.

Find clear stopping and starting shapes using the idea that stillness does not necessarily mean being 'at rest' or 'relaxed'.

Work out phrases of running and stopping using some of the following 'stopping and balancing' words:

wait	hold	settle	perch
freeze	pause	wobble	stop
collapse	stay	hover	linger
balance	rest		

Going and stopping

54

Hover   suspend   freeze

PAUSES

Improvise using position, motion, pause. Create a series of quick, short movements separated by pauses. Experiment freely with timing and rhythm changes. Create a dance based on 'arriving and going' with one or more people, based entirely on the use of pause and the quality of stillness.

SKIPPING EXPLORATIONS

Experiment with skipping forwards, backwards, sidewards and turning. Skip lifting your knees up high. Skip holding hands with a partner – help one another to skip as high off the floor as possible.

SLIDING EXPLORATIONS

Experiment with sliding on different body surfaces, at different speeds and in different directions. Combine sliding with other locomotors, for example run and slide.
Before attempting this make sure that pupils have learnt how to end up on the floor without hurting themselves.

GALLOPING

Gallop forwards, backwards and side-wards. Gallop turning, add an arm circling over your head. Gallop turning with arms straight out at the side. Polka (gallop-gallop-turning-hop) with a partner, holding one another around the waist or holding hands.

HORSES-HORSES

In twos, with one partner in front of the other, both facing the same way; the back partner holds the front partner at the waist. Gallop together, with the front person being the horse and the back person being the rider. Make sure that you both put the same foot down simultaneously.
Allow each partner to have a turn to be the horse.

HOPPING EXPLORATIONS

Practise taking off and rebounding on the same foot. Hop in all directions with the foot in all different positions. Hop holding one leg up.

COMING ACROSS THE FLOOR

Run and hop, with the same leg lifting each time.
Be sure to land softly using your feet to cushion the impact.
Vary your instructions. Ask children to run-run-hop, alternating the lifted or extended leg, with the free leg extended front, back or bent up in front, adding different arm movements and adding a turn or different directions.

Horses-horses

Hopping and jumping are locomotors that travel through space upwards rather than outwards. It is important to teach technique that will prevent injury. Stress pushing away the floor with the toes and stretching the feet in the air, landing softly, going through the feet, making sure knees are bent when landing. Instruct pupils never to land on flat feet or straight legs. Ask the children why this is important.

Run-run-hop

JUMPING EXPLORATIONS

Begin with gentle knee bend bounding, emphasising the alignment of the knees with the middle toes. Add elevation by pushing away the floor with the feet and landing very softly and quietly. Use the arms to assist in jumping higher. Jump from two feet to one foot and one foot to two feet, travelling upwards, sidewards and backwards.

JUMP, HOP AND LEAP

Jump from two feet to two feet, from two feet to one foot and from one foot to two feet; from one foot to the same foot (hopping) and from one foot to the other (leaping). Alternate jumping, leaping and hopping. Identify the difference between them in words.

JUMPING COMPOSITION

Find as many variations as you can and make a fast footwork jump combination. For example combine two fast straight jumps with parallel feet, two fast jumps with half turns, one slower higher jump splitting the legs in the air and one slower, higher jump bending the knees up as high as possible.

Combinations can be made progressively more complicated and challenging by speeding up and by adding arms and head movements.

Teach your combination to a partner and arrange it. Add a run to another spot in the room before repeating the combination. Add a roll (always rounding the spine for protection) and a slide.

Jumping composition

BOUNCING, SPRINGING, EXPLODING

Bouncing ... change shape whilst bouncing ... emphasise rebounding. Springing ... change shape whilst springing ... emphasise defying gravity. Exploding ... change shape one jump at a time ... emphasise the suddenness of the movement. Focus on what the jump feels like. Create a movement sequence where bouncing, springing and exploding jumps and leaps dominate the action.

57

LEAPING EXPLORATIONS

Imagine that you are crossing a river. Leap from rock to rock – low, long leaps. Leap across a bridge.

Use two objects such as shoes, placing them increasingly further apart to encourage greater extensions of the limbs.

Run and leap over an imaginary fence – high leaps.

Place objects in the space for children to leap over. Working in twos, learners find ways to help one another leap higher or further.

Each pair makes a movement sentence combining runs, leaps and hops, or gallops and leaps. Choosing four different locomotors, they compose a short energetic dance.

FLIGHT

Improvise movements using the words fly, soar, swirl, whirl, glide. Emphasise elevation and leaving the floor. Each learner composes a short solo piece based on these words. Join together to develop the solos into a trio. Join two groups together to form a dance for six. Begin the dance with the solos, separate but interrelated in space, followed by the trios and culminating in the sextet.

Leaping across the river

Flying

58

COMBINING LOCOMOTORS

By the Junior Primary stage most children can follow simple instructions combining locomotor movements.

Combine four runs, four skips, run across the space and jump.

These combinations can progressively incorporate direction, level and focus.

LUNGE AND TOUCH

Make a movement sentence – four walks, eight runs, two lunges.

Musically this would be counted as four crotchets, eight quavers and two minims.

Each time you lunge, try to touch someone with your shoulder (or hand, ear, head). Repeat, starting in a large circle and moving inward to the centre of the room. Touch a different person with each lunge.

This exercise combines space awareness, body awareness and locomotors.

Other locomotors

Other locomotor movements are variations of the eight basic locomotors. Explore them, combine them and see what images they produce:

creep	scurry	stride	race
stroll	spring	limp	dodge
march	roll	stalk	strut
amble	meander	scramble	hustle
stagger	crawl	trudge	prance
plod	saunter	slink	hobble

Twist and curl and writhe and stretch

Axial movement

Axial movements take place around or along the spine or axis, for example twist or turn.

Reach and recoil

Twist, drop and undulate

TELEPHONE NUMBERS

Using the combination "open, close, fold, reach, recoil", arrange it to your telephone number. For example, if the first three digits of a telephone number are 4-3-8, do the first movement (open) to four counts or repeated four times. The next movement (close) do for three counts or repeat three times; the next movement, (fold) repeat eight times or once for eight counts, and so on.

AXIAL-LOCOMOTOR COMPOSITION

Select two or three locomotor and two or three axial movement words. Build a composition around these.

This can be done individually or in groups with endless variations and added imagery or restrictions.

DYNAMIC ACTION PHRASES

Explore the dynamic action phrases below.
- swoop, swirl, sink, slide, leap and twirl away
- curl, writhe, twist, unfold, freeze and crumple to the floor
- expand, contract, explode, cascade
- round and round, up and down, sink and roll away.

Create your own dynamic action phrase. Teach it to a partner. Add repetition, and pauses. Try reversing the action.

Using imagery

Exploring movement through story-telling

Tell a story that uses lots of movement words, with pupils being and doing everything in the story. Use the word "imagine" rather than "pretend" so that pupils will experience the story, rather than act it.
   Stories told by the teacher work better with younger pupils. The stories must, however, be suitable for the age and gender. With older students a story may be suggested, such as African tales or 'The Owl and the Pussy Cat' and the pupils can compose a dance using the words, the theme, the idea or the atmosphere. The following movement story was adapted from a drama book by Brian Way (1967:94 – 97) and has been used very successfully with six to eight year olds.

THE MAGIC STONE

Once upon a time you were all fast asleep. Suddenly the alarm bell rings … and you all wake up … but you are very sleepy so you curl up and go right back to sleep. Prrrr .. the alarm goes off again so you stretch and yawn and get up, get dressed, brush your teeth, walk jauntily down the stairs and make your breakfast.

While pupils are busy, walk around and ask individual pupils what they are making for breakfast.

After you've eaten, you wash your dishes *(encouraging independence and good habits)* and you open the door and skip down the path *(adjust to pupils' living conditions)* jump over the wall and set off for a walk. Soon you come to a field with a high wall so you climb up the wall and jump down the other side. Now you are in a forest and lifting your legs high, you run through the long grass until you come to a prickly hedge. Carefully you climb through the hedge. On the other side it is very muddy and you squelch through the mud until you come to a river. In this river there are crocodiles. You hop from boulder to boulder across the river, being very careful not to fall in the water. Once you are on the other side you take a stone, skim it across to the middle of the river and watch the splash and the circles of water rippling outwards in all directions. Suddenly you see a very strange looking stone at your feet. You pick it up and rub off the sand and find yourself turning round and round and growing larger and larger until you become a huge giant. And the giant goes striding through the field and uproots trees and throws them over his/her shoulder. Suddenly the giant sees a shiny stone, picks it up and rubs off the sand, begins to grow smaller and smaller until he/she becomes a tiny baby bird who has never flown before.

The pupils can pick up any number of stones and become different characters, finally becoming themselves again.

Now you realise that it is getting late so you go back across the river, squelch tiredly through the mud, climb through the bush, trudge through the long grass, over the wall and tiredly make your way home. Then you lie down and have a lovely long rest.

CHAPTER 9

Space

*'Space is the 3-D canvas within which the dancer
creates a dynamic image. Breaking it down into component parts brings a
wealth of possibilities for movement exploration'*
(*Blom and Chaplin*)

Movements exists in both time and space. The body has volume, whether in movement or in stillness and fills space in three dimensions. A body is contained by space, and movement changes the space which the body inhabits. The space is also inhabited by other people and objects, and the changing relationships between them, caused by movement, provides everchanging dynamic images. An understanding of the various aspects of space and their effect can contribute to the broadening of movement vocabulary and to an awareness of the impact and significance of the way in which space is used.

The use of space can be personal (close to the body) or general (shared space). People unconsciously structure the space around them. The space immediately surrounding the body is reserved for intimacy. For some people that space is huge and for others it is quite constricted. Intrusion into this personal space by an outsider may cause 'fight' or 'flight'. In some cultures, people are protective of their personal space while in other cultures people are used to being in much closer contact with one another. Exploring one's attitude towards personal space can bring insight into, and develop sensitivity and understanding towards, one's own and others' attitudes to personal space. In poly-cultural societies, this awareness can contribute to the building of inter-cultural tolerance.

Nations fight wars over the sharing of general space. The sharing of space in a dance class is territorialism in microcosm. It provides an opportunity to learn to negotiate, non-verbally, the communal rights to space. For children it needs to be emphasised in the form of a 'NO BUMPING' rule to ensure everyone's safety.

Personal and general space

MAGIC TYPEWRITER (OR COMPUTER OR KEYBOARD)

Use rhythmic music.
Imagine that you are typing a letter. Your typewriter is magical and it suddenly begins to grow. It curves around you and you are sitting in the middle of it. You continue typing. The typewriter grows even larger and fills the space all around you, so you need to use your whole body to type. Now it fills the whole room so that you have to type with your feet, jumping from letter to letter.

PAINTING

Paint a small imaginery portrait in your personal space.
Paint on a larger imaginery canvas with dots and dashes. Create a contemporary wall painting using tubes of paint and your hands. Paint the walls, ceiling and floor of the room as if you have roller-brushes in both hands – in the general space.

GLASS JAR

You are trapped in a tight glass jar (or coke bottle). You can hardly move. Use any part of your body to try to break out – your elbows, the back of your hands, your knees. Suddenly the jar breaks and you feel free, only to find that you are still trapped, but inside a larger jar. Feel the sides, the top, the bottom. Now push against it as hard as you can. Crash! You're out of that jar – but in a larger one.

LIGHTING UP THE SPACE

Use soft atmospheric music.
You have a candle in the palm of each hand. Light up the space around your body – your personal space. Then light up the general space, and then light up one another.

OPPOSITES

Explore the general space alone and in groups through concepts such as:
- near and far
- outside and inside
- centre and periphery
- straight and zigzag
- across and circumference
- narrow and wide

(Photo of filling in the negative spaces appear overleaf.)

Negative space

This is the unoccupied personal space, in between the limbs and around the body, as in the negative of a photograph.

NEGATIVE SPACE

In twos, one person A makes a shape with his/her body. The partner B fits into A's negative space. A then extricates him/herself and fits into B's negative space.
Repeat the activity a number of times and add music for atmosphere.
Working with the whole class, form a long line. A makes a shape. B fits into A's negative space. C fits into B's negative space and so on until the whole class is connected. Then A extricates him/herself and runs to join on at the end of the line and so on.
Do this at increasingly faster speeds to different types of music for hilarious variations.

NEGATIVE SPACES IN EVERYDAY EXPERIENCES

- You are in the supermarket trying to find something in a hurry, dashing along the aisles, winding in amongst the people, pausing, stretching high, balancing on one or both feet, looking over the tops of heads.
- You are at a very busy train station, zigzagging amongst the people, trying to find someone before the train leaves.
- Sprint along a winding promenade avoiding roller bladers, skaters, baby-strollers and tricycles and stopping in statue shapes.
- Create your own 'negative space' story dance in groups of three to five.

Filling in the negative spaces

Direction

Each movement has direction, in the way the mover is facing, or in the way of moving, or both.

Explore moving
- forward
- backward
- horizontal
- vertical
- sideward
- towards/away-from
- diagonal
- up/down

Play directional games such as running, skipping or walking to touch a specified place in the room. Change direction frequently and quickly.

Run fast and when you meet another person or object turn sharply and keep running in a different direction. Alternate moving forward and backward as if you are on a swing. Move sideways, leading with different parts of the body. Move as if you are a wave rolling forward and breaking on the sand, then being sucked back into the sea. Shoot through space horizontally, vertically and diagonally. Focus on a spot in the room. Move towards it and away from it in as many different ways and moods as possible.

DIRECTIONAL COMBINATIONS

Memory for direction and movement may be developed by following simple directional combinations.

Walk three steps forward, two steps back, run six paces to the left, turn around and sit down.

These can become progressively more complicated involving diagonals and far longer instructions. For older pupils repeat the phrase, reversing the order or directions.

DIRECTIONAL JUMPS

Rapidly call out different directions and the students jump and face that way.

Jump to the front, back, left, right, left-diagonal-front, right-diagonal-back and so on.

Work out a fast footwork jump sequence using at least three different directions.

OVER, UNDER, AROUND AND THROUGH

Work in threes inside a hoop or a chalk circle drawn on the floor, in continual motion – each movement must be over, under, around or through.

Try this with other props such as a large box, a car tyre, a bench, a table or chair/s.

Create a landscape using furniture or props and design a journey that travels over, under, around and through. In this journey everyone must be in constant contact in some way and must help one another.

Add an imaginary environment, for example on the mountain, under the sea, on the moon, or a situation for example a wartime escape or rescue mission.

DIRECTIONAL COMPOSITION

Working in twos, threes or larger groups, create a movement sentence that incorporates at least five different directions. Add stillness, levels, variations in speed and so on.

Levels

People vary in their spatial affinities, are more comfortable with, and have a tendency to move in certain relationships to space. In other words, some people favour moving at a low level, while others prefer moving at a middle or high level.

Moving low is about earthiness and gravity. The middle level facilitates travelling movement and is a transition between low and high. The high level is about elevation, flying and defying gravity. Developing an ability to work at all levels presents a great challenge to dancers and is necessary to move beyond one's comfort zone, to develop versatility and to prevent boredom.

Explore moving at a low level:

crawling	sliding	sitting
crouching	dragging	slithering
wriggling	rolling	

at a middle level, between low and high:

kneeling	standing	gliding
travelling		

at a high level:

jumping	skipping	hopping
leaping	flying	

Low, middle and high levels

MOVE AND FREEZE

Run and freeze in any position that is at a low level.

Repeat using middle and high levels.

When the class understands this concept, add shapes to the freeze (e.g. a round shape).

Add eye focus and direction.

Encourage quick changes of level, focus and direction.

CHANGING LEVELS

Explore moving from low to high – a seed growing into a tree or flower – or from high to low – an ice cream melting. In three's improvise together, with each person at a different level constantly or alternating levels.

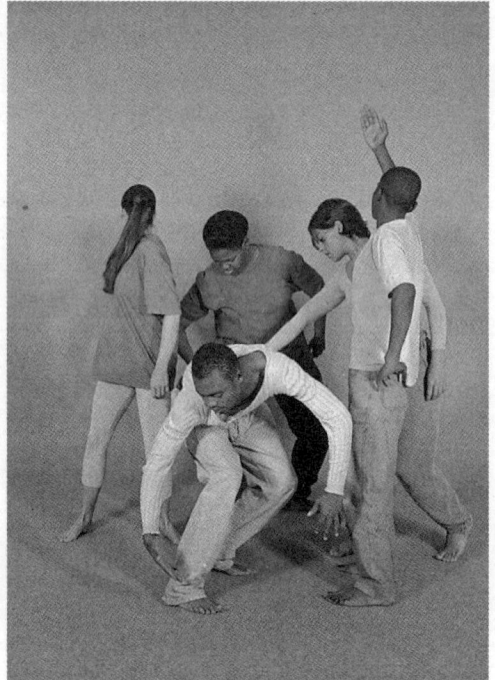

Moving through different levels

68

FLOOR PATTERNS

Imagine that your feet are covered with red paint. As you dance your feet make a red pattern on the floor. Create floor patterns using curved, linear and angular movements. Draw a pattern on a chalkboard, or paper. Design a dance guided by the pattern.

Alternatively, give the students a piece of paper with a pattern already drawn on it and which they must interpret. Examples:

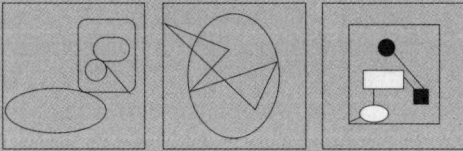

Eye focus

Focus has both dramatic and spatial effect. It is said that the eyes are the windows to the soul. People react to the power of someone's gaze and the abstract space is defined in part by the person's focus. The use of focus affects spatial relationships (near and far), and clarifies direction of movement and attention (single to multi-focus). (See also Chapter 5.)

Explore moving (walking, running and so on) with different types of focus:

wandering	inward	piercing
evasive	distant	flickering
fixed	darting	

DRAW AND REPEL

Begin in a group at one corner of the room. Choose a point of focus and allow it to draw you – as a group.

Repeat the exercise, but this time resist the pull which is ultimately stronger than you are.

As a group choose a focus in the centre of the space. Improvise freely but keeping constantly aware of that focus.

Begin in a tight group. Something frightening (the focus) is repelling you. Fight to remain where you are and together.

INSIDE/OUTSIDE

In groups of five to ten, one person stands in the middle while the others join hands in a circle. The person inside the circle tries to escape and is prevented by the others. Reverse the situation. The person is now on the outside of the circle trying to get in. Let each person have a chance to be inside and outside the circle.

After the activity, lead a discussion with the participants about how the experience felt, what feelings it brought to the surface and what it reminded them of.

Design in space

Design – the shape of one or more bodies in space – can be defined according to the lines of the shape, (curved, linear or angular) and the overall shape (symmetrical or asymmetrical). The different dimensions show a marked and distinctive contrast in their dramatic implications. Curved and circular lines produce a sense of flow and continuity, are graceful and lyrical, yielding, restful, accommodating and organic.

Straight lines and angles give a feeling of power, direction, percussiveness, rigidity. They cut through space and may be more exciting or dynamic than curved movement.

FREEZE SHAPE

On each drum beat make a shape and freeze. Don't think about what shape you are going to make next. Let it be spontaneous. Surprise yourself.

Play the drum faster and faster so that the shapes begin to merge into movement. This is a great ice-breaker exercise. Try it in pairs and larger groups.

TRACING

Make a shape and freeze. Become aware of the details of that shape. Relax. Return to exactly the same shape. In pairs, one person, A, makes a shape; the partner B, with eyes closed, then traces that shape and finally becomes that shape. A checks that B's shape is accurate. Repeat with B making the shape.

SHAPE AND SIZE IDEAS

Move about the space as if you are very wide. Move as if you are travelling through a narrow maze.

Experiment with the size of the movements and the shapes your body makes in space. Alternate large, medium and small movements and shapes.

Connect two body parts (for instance elbow and knee) to form your new shape and travel like that with small movements and then with larger movements.

Freeze shape

Angular shapes

CURVILINEAR, LINEAR AND ANGULAR

Draw circles with your elbows, knees, wrists; draw figure 8's with your ankle, both palms, knees and elbows, use your whole body to travel clockwise and anti-clockwise. How do those movements make you feel? What do you like or dislike about circular movement?

Use your body to make lines in space – horizontal, vertical, diagonal – travel through space in straight lines, travel in zigzag lines. How do straight movements feel? Which feels easier? Why?

Find the angles in your body, chin to neck, elbows and knees, all joints. Explore how many different ways you can make angles. How does this movement feel?

Choose a circular, linear and angular movement and join them together in a movement sentence. In twos, improvise together, with one person emphasising linear movement and the other emphasising circular movement.

In pairs, find ways to propel one another through space.

CIRCULAR

In small groups, work on what can be done with a circle. The circle can revolve clockwise and anti-clockwise. It can expand and contract, with and without a point of focus.

It can travel in either direction whilst opening and closing. It can rise and fall. Body shapes and action within it can be the same, alternate or all be different. They can be in unison, occur one after the other, change fronts, and so on.

Work choreographically, using circles and emphasising axial shapes and movements. Explore the many possibilities. Put two groups together, one inside the other, and explore what is possible with double circles and circles within circles. Create a short, finished sequence that can be performed and repeated.

SHADOWS

Be a shadow on a wall. What shape do you make? Move to the music. Try to imagine what your shadow is doing. In pairs, one person moves while the other shadows them.

GEOMETRIC SHAPES

Individually or in groups, use your bodies to construct a square, a rectangle, a hexagon, and so on. *Connections can be made here with the Maths lessons, introducing children experientially to geometric shapes and then letting them draw and describe the shapes.*

EXPLORING SHAPES THROUGH IMAGERY

How many straight shapes can you think of? (rulers, railway tracks, and so on). See how many straight shapes you can make with your body. How many round shapes can you think of? (balls, the moon, wheels, and so on). How many round shapes can you make with your body? Make a spiky shape. Make a squiggly shape. Turn to the person closest to you and each of you teach the other one your squiggly shape.

CATERPILLAR

Tell a story that incorporates the shape concept.
Crawl like a caterpillar on the ground (long, thin shape). Take a thread and spin yourself into a cocoon (small, round shape). Grow wings so that the cocoon becomes spiky. Break out of the cocoon and fly freely as a butterfly.

WHAT SHAPE ARE YOU?

• Blow yourself up like a balloon. Grow larger and larger until you pop. Now what shape are you?
• You are inside an egg. Slowly you push against the shell of the egg until you suddenly break through. What shape are you now?
• In groups of three, join yourselves together to form a monster. How does this monster move? What kinds of sounds does it make? Working together, create a monster dance.

Making round shapes

72

SCRIBBLES

Draw a scribble pattern in the air with your hand, then imitate the pattern using your whole body.

Paint the air with different body parts, paint with your whole body – large, slow strokes of paint, alternating with spurts and dashes, or fine, thin, slow, careful lines.

In groups make a moving collage, each person creating their own pattern and finding a way to work them together to make one overall design.

WORD DANCE

In groups of three to five, form a word-statue with each person portraying a single letter. Lets see whether we can read your word.

This can be developed into a language lesson, for example, how many other words can you make with those same letters? Express the meaning of your word in movement. Now create a dance that begins with the word-statue, moves to the word meaning and ends back in the word-statue.

GROUP CIRCLE

Form a large circle. One person runs into the centre and forms a shape.The next person runs to the centre and forms another shape attached to the first person and so on until all are involved. Then, keeping your shape, bounce (or make other movement) back to the outer circle.

The same can be done in straight line with each person joining on to the previous one. Variations can be added by each person changing the shape of the person they join.

ALPHABET EXPLORATIONS

Explore ways of shaping the body into alphabet shapes, either upper or lower case. Use your whole body.Try an 'e', a 'c', a 'j'. Trace letter shapes in the air, using different body parts. Make floor patterns using letter shapes, for example make a 'm' floor design.

Alphabet explorations

Symmetry and asymmetry

Symmetry, in which the design is exactly the same on both sides of centre, produces a feeling of strength and authority, stability, balance, predictability and control. Asymmetry, on the other hand, inherently possesses and produces tension and a dynamic quality. 'Even in stillness, an asymmetrical design has a pull and thrust or weightedness in some direction. Because of this, it implies movement, it projects excitement.' (*Blom and Chaplin, 1982:39*)

While symmetrical movement is safe, asymmetrical movement is risky. It may give a sense of being off-centre, unpredictable, funny, tortuous, complex or distorted. Because dance is about moving, about dynamism, its moments of excitement and highest interest tend to be asymmetrical with symmetry being used for contrast, rest or closure.

SCULPTURES

Each working alone with eyes closed, sculpt an imaginary shape. Now become that shape and freeze.
Select four examples, two that are symmetrical and two that are asymmetrical, and elicit from the rest of the class what the differences are. Now create two symmetrical and two asymmetrical shapes, join them together, in any order and add transitions from one shape to the next. Vary the speed, level and direction of the transitions. In pairs, teach one another, join the two movement sentences and arrange them.
Now using two bodies, create four symmetrical and asymmetrical shapes, joining them and developing the transitions between each shape.

Environment

The environment is an integral part of the dance and affects how one moves. Using a variety of environments, actual and imaginary, provides a rich source of inspiration and material. Dance classes may take place inside or outside, in school halls, in classrooms filled with desks, or on the school playground or field. Many schools lack facilities. Teachers have to use what is available to them. Besides the obvious spaces, out-of-the-ordinary environments can be exciting and inspiring. Try designing a class for an adventure playground, park, local art gallery, church, gymnasium, university campus or foyer of a shopping mall (only for the very uninhibited!)

Create your own environment: cover the floor with leaves, sand, ping-pong balls, ladders, chairs, cardboard boxes, newspaper, fabric – the possibilities are infinite. Create imaginary environments to use for improvisations, for example the beach, underwater, on the planet Mars, on a narrow mountain path, in a forest, in a dense fog, trapped by a fire or in a prison cell.

ENVIRONMENT EXPLORATIONS

Explore your environment. Trace the shapes and mould yourself against the shapes. Express the shapes in movement. Allow the spaces to suggest and manipulate your movements.

PLAYGROUND

Use an imaginary playground (swings, see-saws, slides and so on) for exploring movements using gravity and momentum.

ACTION STORY

Make up an action story across a desert, over a mountain, or underground in the mines.

JOURNEY

Choose a space where you feel comfortable. Let this be your home base. Choose another spot and walk there. Be in that space for a while and see how the view differs from there. Repeat with a third spot. Return to your home base. Travel the same route a number of times.

Think about the places you go to on a regular basis, for example from home to class to the supermarket and back home. Think how you feel when you travel to each of those places: are you enthusiastic or reluctant? Do you travel fast, slow or at a normal pace?

Find a movement that expresses the feelings for each route of your journey. Travel your route a number of times. If on your journey someone gets in your way, negotiate a solution, pass them or join them for a while or permanently. See how others influence your journey.

Follow this activity with a discussion about what you became aware of during this exercise.

THE JUNGLE

You are in a very dense jungle, surrounded by lots of giant plants, trees and bushes, moving through the deep dark undergrowth, slithering and sliding. Huge leaves curl and uncurl, threatening to envelope you.

Now imagine that you are the huge leaves uncurling and spreading (starting in the hands and growing through the body) and then shrivelling and dying.

As yourself again, move over thorny bushes, around tall, dark tree trunks and become caught in a tangle of branches. Suddenly there is a summer storm ... the rain beats down, causing the mud to swirl at your feet ... you manage to break free and twist and thrash your way out of the jungle to the dangerous swamps.

Carefully you tread through the swamp lifting your feet high with every step as the mud sucks you down. You struggle to reach for a hanging branch. You see a crocodile approaching and quickly manage to pull yourself along the branch, up into the overhanging tree – only to come face to face with a huge python! You freeze in terror with no way to turn. From a distance you hear the sound of an approaching helicopter, see the hanging ladder swinging towards you – rescue at last! You grab the bottom rung of the ladder and swing off to safety.

CHAPTER 10

Time

Movement is the manifestation of energy in time and space.

Energy, as we experience it in the movements of our own bodies, is not expressed in a steady smooth stream, but as a succession of impulses. An impulse is a wave of energy that rises from rest to a peak and falls back to rest. One impulse tends to create another. It is the wave-like nature of the impulse, the alternation of activity and rest which we experience as rhythm.

Rhythm is a difficult concept to define because it is open to a variety of interpretations. Our understanding of rhythm is that it is a recognisable flow of movement and/or sound. The word 'rhythm' originates from an ancient Greek word – 'rhio', meaning 'to flow'.

One perceives rhythm in movement kinesthetically, in the relationship of time and energy. Rhythm is intrinsic in all human and environmental movement – ocean waves, the flight of birds, the heartbeat, breathing. Many rhythms, especially natural ones, are not necessarily regular, repetitive, predictable or steady. Rhythms can be irregular, unpredictable and jagged too. A rhythmic pattern, on the other hand, is a clearly defined pattern of time aspects such as duration and accent. The more regular and obvious the relationship pattern of time to energy, the more easily one is able to recognise and define the rhythm. The ability to use rhythm in different ways can enhance and broaden improvisation and choreographic ingenuity.

Aspects of time

Aspects of time which apply to movement are:
- *beat or pulse* – the regular, constant throb – a measure of the passing of time
- *tempo* (speed) – the rapidity of pulses; the tempo may be fast, slow, accelerating or decelerating
- *pace* – the rate at which an activity proceeds
- *duration* – the amount of time taken; a fast movement has a short duration and a slow movement has a long duration
- *accent* – an emphasis or stress
- *syncopation* – the displacement of the regular metrical accent to a weak beat or between beats; it can also be understood as the delaying or speeding up of a beat
- *climax* – the accumulated high point
- momentum – impetus gained by movement: qualifying factors are mass and velocity during the transference of weight
- *bar* – unit of counts
- *meter* – the number of beats in a bar
- *time signature* – the sign indicating the grouping of pulses into equal time units
- *phrase* – a short and more or less independent passage forming part of a longer passage or piece; the smallest and simplest unit of form which has a beginning, a middle and an end forming part of a larger whole; a phrase has form and content and the movements in a phrase share a common element of intent
- *rhythmic forms* – the shape, arrangement,

mode or proportion which provide the structure on which compositions are built, for example, canon, rondo, theme and variations.

• *musicality* – the observance of dynamics in sound and movement in a logical, expressive and understandable manner

• *style* – a mode of expression and execution, a distinct set of characteristics consistently applied.

The following samples give an indication of how some of these abstract concepts can be experienced:

Rhythm

NAME PATTERNS

Stand in a circle. Going around the circle each person claps out the rhythmic pattern of his/her name once, followed by the whole group copying the rhythm and saying the name. Repeat, but this time each person reproduces his/her name pattern in movement.
This is an excellent ice-breaking exercise for a new class who do not know one another.

AFRICAN POLY-RHYTHMS

Clap five beats accenting the first and third beats – (a). Then clap five beats accenting the second and fourth beats – (b). Half the group claps the (a) rhythm and the other half claps the (b) rhythm at the same time. Develop this using any number of beats, any number of groups and any type of movement.
Poly-rhythms can be used to teach mathematics concepts – see Chapter 15.

GROUP JOG

Form a group. Each person puts a hand on the shoulder of the person in front so that the whole group is connected. Choose a leader who has a good sense of rhythm. The leader starts jogging in time to a metered rhythm – preferably a piece of music, but a drum can be used – with the group falling into the rhythm.

As a variation, lose direct physical contact with each other but maintain the rhythm. The group, joined or apart, forms a swarm of bees or insects, a herd of animals, or a flock of birds and continues to move together, in the same rhythm or in a different one.

This exercise is useful to establish rhythm and a group feeling – particularly useful when students cannot pick up a specific rhythm.

FIND YOUR OWN MOVEMENT RHYTHM

The teacher plays a rhythm on a drum. Listen to the drum. Now move any way you want to the drum. Keep moving to the drum.
The teacher plays regular and irregular phrases and the pupils move.
Now keep moving but listen to the rhythm in your head or hum your own rhythm.

GROUP ORCHESTRAS

Choose an 'instrument' from everyday items (a show, a bunch of keys, a ruler, a box). Using your 'prop-instrument', set up a rhythm individually and then co-ordinate your rhythms to form an 'orchestra'. Select one person at a time to conduct the orchestra.

Let half of the class become the dancers who move to the sounds of the orchestra and then switch around.

Rhythmic patterns

KNEE PATTERNS

Sit in a circle all patting your knees. The leader claps a rhythm and all copy. Each person gets a turn to make up a different rhythm, continuing to clap it until all have mastered it. Keep the patterns very simple.

This is a good listening exercise.

REGULAR AND IRREGULAR RHYTHMIC PATTERNS

Stamp out a regular rhythmic pattern with your feet. Now stamp out an irregular series. Discuss the different effects produced.

LISTEN AND CLAP

Listen to a piece of music with a regular beat. Clap the regular beat, then clap across the beat in an irregular rhythm. Listen to music that does not seem to have a regular rhythmic pattern. Try to define rhythm and rhythmic pattern.

COMPLEX RHYTHMIC PATTERNS

Walk to a steady beat of 12 counts, establishing a straight or curved pathway. Somewhere during the '1-count' phrase set a movement that lasts three counts ... use some of the counts in a low movement ... a turn ... an elevation ... a movement diagonally backwards ... an accent in two places ... a movement diagonally upwards and forwards ... a rhythmic pattern that is pronounced. Each movement must be added in the order given and all movements need to be maintained regardless of new ones added. Give the sequence an unusual ending.

Rhythmic patterns

PULSE

Stand in a circle. One person establishes a pulse by clapping. All join in, clapping in unison. Be careful not to speed up or slow down. The person who initiated the impulse stops. Then everyone stops. The next person claps a new pulse and the procedure is repeated.

Variations: add a movement to the clap, and add travel with alternating leaders. Experiment with double-speed or half-speed.

RHYTHM AND RHYME

Give one student a rhyme and read aloud. Stand on the spot, chant the rhyme, clap the rhyme and stamp the rhyme. Find ways to move about the space, chanting, clapping and stamping. Remove the words once the rhythm is established and create a new, original rhyme using the same rhythmic pattern.

TEMPO

Experiment with speed, for example walking very slowly as if you've got a stomach-ache; walk fast as if you can't wait to get home; accelerating – as if you're a car and you start slowly and get faster and faster, the fastest you can … and then less fast, slower, and slower until you stop; slowly sink to the ground and slowly come up following your shoulder, drop fast, jump up fast, and so on.

VARIATIONS IN TIMING

Compose a short dance. Elicit differences in qualities of movement by varying the timing of the whole dance or of parts of the dance. For example, begin slowly and speed up to a climax; vary the speed and add repetition of certain sections or movements.

PACE

Use this activity to teach pace and sensitivity to one another.
In twos, walk behind your partner. Put the same foot down as he or she does (right or left) at exactly the same time. Each partner has a chance to lead. Do the same walking next to one another with one leading then with neither leading, but keeping pace with each other.

ACCENT

Play the drum and ask the class to walk in time to the beat.
Clap on each step, then clap on every second, then stamp on every third step (still walking). Run in three-time patterns   123 / 123 / 123. Stamp on 1 as you're running. Make 1 stronger any way you want. For example, use an arm or head movement. Walking, clap on the first of every four beats. Running, stamp on the first of every five steps. Walk in a five beat rhythm, emphasising the first and fourth beat in any way you wish.
Vary accent and locomotors in many ways.

10-seconds movements

DURATION

Make one movement that lasts
10 seconds (teacher times it). Make
ten movements that together last
10 seconds. See how many movements you can make in 10 seconds.
Make 25 movements in 10 seconds.

SYNCOPATION

Compose a series of movements that
can be repeated. Play with the speed
by doing them in slow motion, at
double speed, experimenting with
delaying and speeding up movements, (lengthening and shortening
the duration of the movement) and
changing the accent. Try this in
groups of two or more, each accenting
different parts of the movement
phrase.

CLIMAX

Compose a complete series of movements, a short dance that can be
repeated. Experiment with making one
part more dominant or more significant –
create a climax to the dance by organis-
ing the material to emphasise one part.
Keep changing the climax point by:
• increasing the tempo
• enlarging the movement range
• adding more dancers
• increasing the movement dynamics
• suspending the movement altogether
for a moment.

MOMENTUM

Discuss the concept of momentum.
Experiment with different degrees of
power and speed. Work with weight
and tempo in pairs exploring how to
increase momentum.

BAR / METER / TIME SIGNATURES

Sit in a circle with a piece of paper and a pencil each. Clap 16 regular beats. Represent the beats on paper as in Morse code:

– – – – – – – – – – – – – – – –

Clap harder on the 1st, 5th, 9th, 13th beats. Repeat this a few times. Represent this on paper in Morse code as:

/–––/–––/–––/–––// This represents four bars of four counts or 4/4.

Stamp the pattern and then compose a movement sentence in this pattern.

Explore basic time signatures using movement. Clap and move to a 2/4, 3/4, 4/4, 5/4 and 6/8 rhythm.

When movement phrases are choreographed in the course of the class, encourage experimentation by using different time signatures for the same combination.

TIME PATTERNS

On a piece of paper design a time pattern, for example:

––––/––––/––––/––––
––––––––/––––––––
♩♩♩♩♩♩♩♩
––––/––––/––––

First sing 'la-la' your time pattern for duration, and then clap it repeatedly until you know it without looking at the paper.

The whole class claps the time pattern while the pattern composer improvises freely.

Work out a movement phrase for each line of your time pattern, and join the movement phrase for each line together to make a longer sequence.

PHRASING

In pairs, one person, A, makes a movement phrase and freezes. B copies the freeze pose and performs the next phrase and freezes. A then adopts B's pose and performs the next phrase, and so on.

A performs a question movement phrase and freezes; B performs an answering movement phrase and freezes.

In pairs, move to alternate phrases of the music – A moves to the first phrase and freezes while B moves to the next phrase.

Rhythmic form and structure

CANON

In groups of four, students arrange themselves in single file with the person at the front being the leader. Choose a time signature. For example in 4/4 time, the leader moves continuously to the music. The second in line imitates the leader, starting four counts later. The third person watches the second person and imitates four beats later, and so on. Change leadership until everyone has had a turn to lead. A round is an on-going canon.

RONDO

Form a movement phrase A. Add on a new phrase B then repeat A – ABA. Or add on a different variation C, and repeat A, and so on ABACADA.

THEME AND VARIATIONS

Create a strong movement phrase (the theme). Keep using the same theme but develop it by varying the tempo, rhythm, style, level, direction, and so on. The theme is A, followed by A1, A2, A3, A4 and so forth.

SING THE RHYTHM

Create a short dance. Teach it to a partner. Rather than counting, sing the rhythm as you move.

STYLE

Discuss different styles and forms of dances. Identify what aspects of time and rhythm influence style. In groups of three to five, compose a dance in a specific style. Perform the dance for the class. The class identifies what stylistic elements of time were used.

During a creative class, try to use as many different forms and qualities of music as possible. Encourage students to create their own rhythms instead of relying on recorded music.

CHAPTER 11

Force

Every movement involves time, space and force.

In any movement, it is energy that provides the 'go' power. Energy is the potential for force, the capacity for action and for overcoming resistance or gravity. The amount of energy used, the intensity of the energy exerted, expended or released, determines the force (or effort) of the movement.

The way in which energy is released and force is exerted determines the quality or feeling of the movement. The quality of movement in dance is like colour in painting and harmony in music. It is the dynamic quality in dance that speaks to the emotions. The quality of movement is produced by the dynamic interaction of force (energy) with time in space. The elements of time, space and force cannot be separated except for discussion. One cannot make a single movement without using each one, and all simultaneously.

The awareness of these elements and their effect on each other leads to an awareness of the possibilities of the art of dance. A wider range of movement experiences will be opened to students as they acquire the ability to vary aspects of force in a skilful and sensitive manner.

All movement can be altered by changes in force, depending on the amount of energy used, how it emerges (sharply or smoothly), the weight (heavy or light), and the flow (jerky or continuous).

The following activities and images give experiences of the different ways of using force.

LIGHT AND SUDDEN

- Tap a Morse code message
- Be a drop of water dripping from the tap
- Flick insects off you
- Pat the fire out

LIGHT AND SUSTAINED

- Float like a glider
- Skate on thin ice
- Ooze out of a tube of tooth paste
- Melt like an ice cream on a hot day
- Drift on a lilo on the water

STRONG AND SUSTAINED

- Lock hands – pull apart
- Squeeze the laundry
- Press elbows together
- Drag a fishing net up the beach
- Push a piano up the stairs
- Pull the dog on a leash
- Knead the bread

Strong and sudden

STRONG AND SUDDEN

Kick your feet in all directions.
- Thrust your knees in all directions (forward, backward, upward, sideward).
- Be a ball that is being thrown.
- A helicopter is dropping R20 notes – grab as many as you can.
- Chop down a tree.
- Stamp in the sand.

Ask questions to make the children think about what they are doing:
What do you need to help you chop the tree and kick the ball?
  Answer – energy.
How does the energy come out?
  Answer – strongly and suddenly.

PHRASES

Compose four contrasting movement phrases:
- a strong percussive phrase
- a strong sustained phrase
- a light percussive phrase
- a light sustained phrase

Use these phrases in two, creating an action-reaction dance.

CONTRASTS

Explore contrasts of force by improvising around these words:
- explode, punch, whip (strong and sudden)
- press, wring, pull (strong and sustained)
- glide, float, skate (light and sustained)

Contrasts – push and pull

Tension and relaxation

Movement can be forceful (powerful, energetic), or forceless (energyless), active (self-initiated) or passive (non-self-initiated), tense (trapped energy) or relaxed (released energy). The whole range of body movement exists on a continuum between the opposite poles of tension and relaxation. Extreme tension causes rigidity and extreme relaxation causes inertia. At each of these opposite poles there is stillness.

OPPOSITE POLES OF MOVEMENT

Lie down on the floor and relax completely. Be completely relaxed … no tension anywhere in the body … no movement … inert. Gradually bring your entire body to a state of complete tension with every muscle so tight you can't move anymore … hold for a moment and then let go all the tension returning to your state of complete relaxation.

Change the dynamic pattern by suddenly becoming completely tense, gradually release the tension until you are completely relaxed … gradually tense, suddenly relax. Each time you tense or relax find a new position. Let the movement towards tension move you around the room … as you release the tension, allow the movement to take you somewhere else.

Explore forceful movements which are strong and powerful. Contrast these with forceless movements, very weak, little energy. Continue to move as if you are being moved by some outer force. Move as if you are a puppet and someone else is controlling the strings, as if moved by a strong gale, as if you are a rag doll being thrown by a child. Try the opposite: be a moving force, active.

How did this feel? Which one did you prefer? Active or passive?
Explore other opposite poles of movement such as:
- percussive, sustained,
- strong, weak
- smooth, jerky,
- tight, loose
- soft, hard,
- gradual, sudden

ACTIVE AND PASSIVE

In twos, one of you is active and the other is passive. The active partner tests the passive one, to see if the person is really able to be moved by an outer force.

Passivity is not the same as relaxation – the passive partner cannot be totally relaxed or they will be a dead weight and difficult to move. They should be relaxed enough to sense the force exerted on them, but light and flexible enough to be easily moved.

Reverse roles and do the same again. Try this in threes with one person active and the other two passive.

Active person: draw the passive ones together, push them apart, lead them, drive them, use your whole body to move them. Your movements should express powerfulness. Theirs should reflect powerlessness.

Try this in a larger group with one active person manipulating the group.

RELAXATION

Imagine that you are:
- a wax candle slowly melting
- a snowman at the end of winter
- a slab of butter standing in the sun
- an ice cream cone melting in the sun

PASSING THE POWER BACK AND FORTH

In pairs improvise alternating the roles of active and passive partner following on from the exercise above, changing over roles at the end of each movement phrase.

Try this holding hands and without holding hands. Then let the force flow freely back and forth between you. Vary your movements as much as you can.

Try the same in a group of three. Let the movement determine who is the active one. Don't be afraid to assume leadership if your position in the movement indicates that you should.

JELLY-JOINTED

In groups of three, one person is jelly-jointed or in a state of collapse and the other two have to hold him/her up. What is her/his relationship to gravity? How does active energy deal with gravity? What would happen if we all give in to gravity constantly?

PERCUSSIVE, SUSTAINED, FAST AND SLOW

Respond in movement to these images:
• a machine gun (percussive-fast) shooting down a jet plane (sustained-fast)
• a person with hiccups (percussive-slow) walking on the moon (sustained-slow)
• an automatic Morse Code transmitter gone haywire, sending erratic, rapid and infrequent messages (percussive-fast mixed with percussive-slow)
• a speedy slithering snake (sustained-fast), then a slow hunting snake (sustained-slow)

WEIGHT

Imagine that you are lifting a very heavy weight; use your whole body to lift it. Then lift something that is as light as a feather; lift it rapidly above your head. Push something very heavy away from you; use your arms, your back, your legs, your whole body. Flick something light away from you; flick it with different parts of your body.

Now do all the strong movements you can think of … movements with weight behind or in front. Find movements to do that feel heavy. Move through the air as if it is heavy.

Try skipping, jumping and leaping as if you are carrying heavy weights and being pulled down by gravity. Now try skipping, jumping and leaping as if you are weightless, like on the moon where there is no gravity to pull you down.

Improvise freely, contrasting heavy and light movements.

POW-ZOWIE-ZAM

Create a solo dance sequence from the phrase POW-ZOWIE-ZAM, or a similar phrase, using powerful dynamic actions. Perform it at normal speed, twice as slow and twice as fast.

Perform it again in a very restricted space and again using as much space as possible. Perform it with as much strength as possible and then with delicacy. Finally develop the sequence into a dance using the same phrase in as many different ways as possible.

ENERGY BALL

Imagine that you have a ball of energy in your hand. Send it along your arm up to your shoulder, across your chest to your other shoulder, diagonally down across your torso to your hip, down your leg to your foot and kick it back up to catch it in your belly button. Try this with your eyes closed but keeping a strong focus (internally without using your eyes) on the path of the energy ball. If the energy ball leaves your body, let it still be attached by an invisible thread.

PUPPET ON A STRING

In twos, begin with one person lying down, as if a puppet. The partner, like a puppeteer, controls the actions of the puppet by controlling the invisible strings attached to different parts of the body. The puppet-person responds to the lightest touch of the puppeteer-person. After a while, change over roles.

SPAGHETTI RELAXATION

Imagine that you are like raw spaghetti: stiff, standing in a pot. As the water begins to boil you begin to soften, slowly, until you are completely soft, swishing around in the rapidly boiling water.

POPCORN

Curl up on the floor as if you are a small kernel of corn. What happens when the oil begins to heat? The corn begins to swell until it begins to pop. As the music begins, explore the feeling of moving from small and curled to large and jumping.

COLOUR

Think about the colour blue. What things can you think of that are blue?
  How does blue make you feel? What words would you use to describe blue? Improvise around the idea of blue … be blue, express what blue means to you. Explore other colours:
• *cool colours:* green, silver
• *warm colours:* gold, red, orange, yellow
• *sombre colours:* black, dark blue, grey, dark brown
  How do these colours influence the way energy is released? Which colours invite the use of slow, light, lyrical qualities? Which inspire quick-strong and quick-light qualities or strong-slow dynamic qualities?

RAINBOW DANCE

In groups of seven, each person chooses one colour of the rainbow and creates a movement phrase to reflect the atmosphere which that colour evokes. Join the movement phrases together to create a rainbow dance.

Swinging

Because of the mechanical structure of the human body, swinging is the most frequently used movement quality as well as the most natural, like throwing or hitting a ball. The swing can be analysed as an initial application of force which is then released as the movement reacts to the pull of gravity and the effect of momentum. The final part of the swing is usually checked and this leads to a slight pause between consecutive swings and a more controlled movement. The swing is thus composed of
• a slight impulse
• a giving away to gravity
• an unchecked follow-through along the path of an arc
• a momentary suspension before repetition.

SWINGS WITH STRETCHES

Explore swinging with different parts of your body, alone and in combination.
  For example, swing your head from side to side. (Make sure your neck is relaxed or you will get a sore neck). Swing your head and upper torso. Find a swinging movement you like.
  Explore stretching your arms in all directions.
  Put together four swings followed by four stretches, perform two of each and then one of each: swing – stretch – swing – stretch and so on.

SWING DUET

In twos, make up a swinging phrase of eight counts.
  Perform it face-to-face, back-to-back and side-by-side. Add transitions of four or eight counts from one formation to the next or go against a regular beat and make the transitions five or seven beats. Let the transitional movements have a completely different quality.

Swings

COMBINING SWINGS, PERCUSSIVE AND SUSTAINED MOVEMENTS

1. Swings

Experiment with swinging your arm, your leg, your head. Allow swinging to take you across space. Create a travelling, swinging sequence for four counts.

2. Percussive

Throw your head, freeze. Repeat this a few times throwing in all directions. Throw your head and arms, freeze. Throw your head, arms, torso, freeze. Add the legs. Throw yourself across space, freeze.

Do these many times, being spontaneously different each time.

3. Sustained

Stand quietly and contemplate your thumb. Very smoothly, focusing totally on your thumb, move your hand across your body to the other side. Now focus on a different part of your body and move it in a sustained movement. Allow your focus to change to any part of your body that is moving.

4. Combine

Put together four swings travelling across space; four percussive throws ending in a freeze with each one; move slowly and sustainedly for eight counts and freeze. In twos, stand far apart and face one another. Perform your sequence towards and around one another. Try the same with the whole class standing in a circle and moving in towards the centre.

CHAPTER 12

Movement invention

The number of ways of stimulating movement invention is infinite. In addition to the ways suggested in the other chapters, the range of movement can be increased and new movements stimulated through ideas, thoughts, feelings, imagery, natural phenomena, a wide variety of music, props, costumes and everyday objects and activities with which the pupils are familiar. For example, depending upon how it is done, adding an image may make a movement more intensive and interesting.

The use of imagery while teaching is however a contentious issue. According to Spurgeon (*1991:135*) the use of imagery has "the ability to render participant students embarrassed, alienated or uncontrollable". He draws special attention to types of imagery that render a class non-productive and alienating:

• 'Be a tree' type of activity, where the students are told to be something other than what/who they are. Spurgeon claims that this type of exercise elicits stereo-typed responses and embarrassment.

• 'The movement story', where the teacher tells a story while the student interprets the story in movement. Spurgeon maintains that this puts the student into mental overload, faced with a stream of instructions leading to half-hearted attempts to respond that lean towards amateur mime and stereotypic dance.

• 'Emotions on demand', where students are expected to perform an activity with a specific feeling. There is a difference in portraying an abstract emotion in dance and feeling an actual feeling as a result of dance.

While these arguments are worth noting, imagery used carefully and with sensitivity can be very helpful, especially when working with younger learners.

One needs to respect students' social, emotional and intellectual stage of development with regard to the language that is used. Spurgeon suggests using similes rather than metaphors, for example 'Move softly and silently as if you were a tiger stalking its prey' rather than 'Be a tiger stalking your prey' (*1991: 138*). Students should be encouraged to evolve their own imagery.

> **IMAGING**
>
> Walk around the room and every five or ten seconds try a droop, a whirl or a collapse. How does this make you feel? Do you have any pictures in your head? Try moving according to these pictures. If you get stuck, go back to droop, whirl and collapse. Experiment with action words droop, whirl, collapse. Provide your own imagery as you move.
> (From *Spurgeon, 1991: 138*)

Animals

Animal movements encourage the use of the spine. Cats for instance provide a range of different actions involving the spine – arching, stretching, rolling, curling – which can be performed with varying qualities of speed, tension and continuity in different directions and levels. A study of animal movements can stimulate movement invention and can contribute to pupils' understanding of animal habits and behaviour required in other subjects such as Natural Sciences. Exploration of animal movement can be introduced through discussion, looking at pictures of animals and listening to animal stories.

Gesture

ABSTRACTING FROM GESTURE

Explore the gesture for 'Hi' using one hand, then with both hands … changing level … adding a turn and level change … adding a step and direction change. Repeat with (for example) pain … show where the pain is … with sound accompaniment (ooooo) … exaggerate the movement … use stretching movements or twisting movements.

Try this with:

- I like you
- I don't care
- I hate you
- Go away
- Please

In each case start with the gesture and move into the abstract.

IMPULSE, IMPETUS, IMPACT

Begin a movement and then arrest the movement mid-action. Explore many ways of initiating a movement or identify what the word impulse means. Then allow the impetus of the movement to run its course until it is as if you have hit a wall (impact). Explore what happens if you leave out impetus and explore impulse-impact.

Experiment with impulse, impetus, impact. Feel the climax of the movement.

Props

Pupils in their pre- and early teens feel self-conscious about their changing bodies. The use of props at this time is, therefore, especially suitable because it provides the opportunity to move the focus away from the body and onto the object. Introducing a variety of props can extend the range of movement and stimulate new movement. One of the lesson plans in Chapter 4 describes an activity with hoops, for example. The list of props that can be used is endless. Here are a few ideas:

chairs	scarves	hoops	tables
elastics	balloons	hats	ropes
tyres	bench	string	tins
bean-bags	sticks	newspaper	

TINS

Make sounds by banging two empty tins together, or against the floor. See what rhythms you can create. Let your whole body be part of making the sounds. Put together a sequence of movement and tin-sound rhythms.

Teach them to a partner and arrange them together.

Let two groups join their rhythms together, until you have a whole class rhythm dance.

IMAGINARY ROPE

Move as if you are hauling in a boat with a rope. Imagine the strain in the hands, face, body. Lasso with the rope, whirl it around your head and throw it far. Tie it in a knot. Wind it around your elbow. Have a tug or war, pulling back or staggering forward. Feel its strength and its texture. What else can you do with rope?

CHAIR-SHELL

Explore your chair as if it is a huge shell – once you crawl in, you come out in an underwater world.

CHAIRS

Place chairs well spaced around the room. Run in amongst the chairs and when the music stops, freeze on a chair with your feet off the ground.

Repeat a number of times, varying the freeze positions in relation to the chair:

- below
- greedy for
- touching
- challenging of
- afraid of
- admiring of
- repelled by
- possessive of
- loving towards
- glued to

Play with your chair. Turn it upside down or on its side. Use it as a play-pen, as a boat, as a chariot, as a prison cell. Relate to the chair as an old person, as a middle aged person, and as a young person.

CHAIR DANCE

Sit on a chair with your feet off the ground. Find five different positions or shapes on the chair, without your feet touching the floor. Join these together with movement, paying attention to the transitions between positions. Perform your sequence very fast (without falling off your chair).

Freeze on chairs

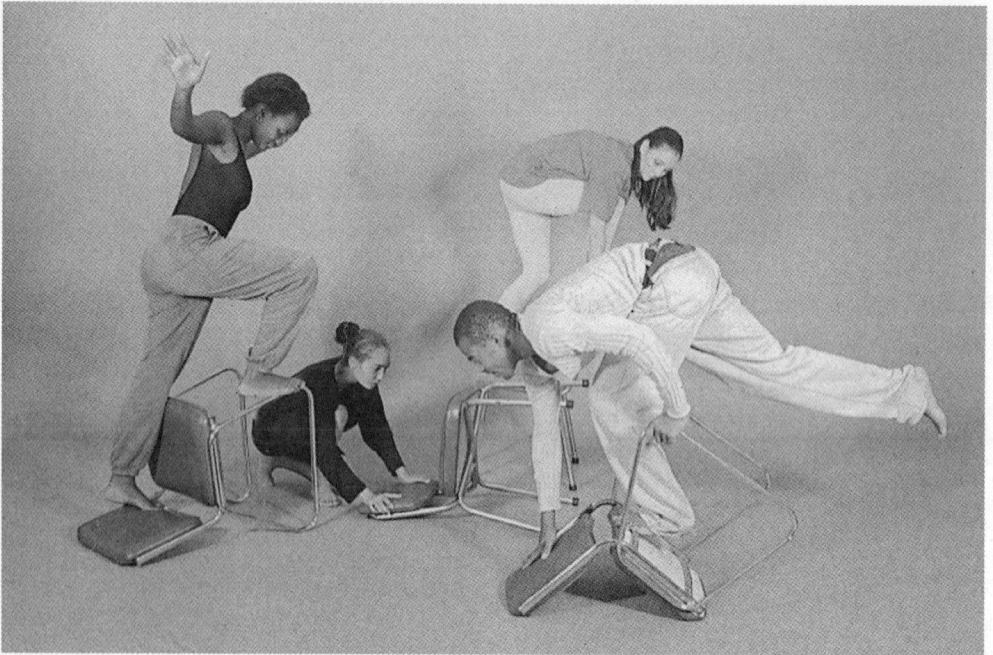

94

NEWSPAPER

Give each pupil a sheet of newspaper.
Crumple your sheet of newspaper into a tight ball. Play with it. Throw it, kick it, roll it, blow it from one hand to another, blow it along the floor, move it with your nose, your elbows, your toes.

Smooth it out and use it as a surf board, as a bull fighter's cloak, as a shelter.

By now the pupils probably need a new sheet of paper.
In twos, one pupil does activities with the paper – rolling the paper down, folding one corner, dropping the paper, throwing it up into the air – while the other person mirrors the movement.

Choose one word that catches your eye from your sheet of newspaper. Create a movement phrase that expresses that word. In twos each show your movement to your partner while the partner guesses what the word was. Let the class see these movement phrases and guess what the word was.

Use as much newspaper as you need to create an impromptu costume. Find a movement that suits your costume. Following one after the other, promenade in your costumes each doing your particular movement.

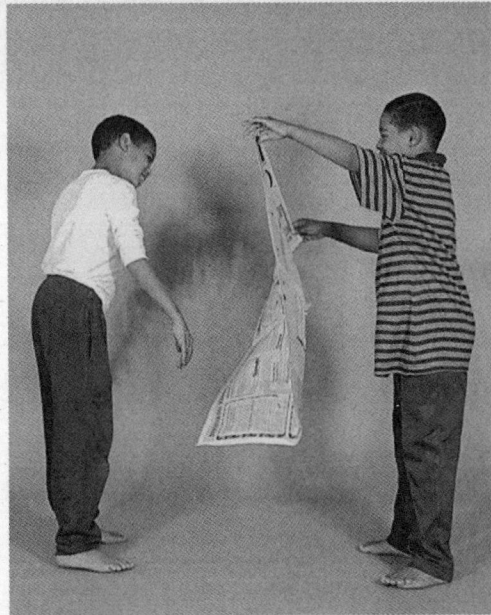

Newspaper dance

COSTUMES

Create a character by putting on a hat or a cape, or picking up a cane.

Decide who your character is and how s/he moves. Join a partner and work out in movement how the two characters relate to one another.

BALLS

Bounce an imaginary ball. Move as if you are the ball that is being bounced, kicked, rolled and thrown.

In twos, place a real large ball between your bodies. Move as much as you can, maintaining the ball between the two bodies without using your hands.

95

BOXES

Move in relation to the box:

towards	away	around
through	under	over
as if it's not there		bottom to top

Hold your box and dance with it in any way that you wish. Take it high and low, make circles with it, shake it.

Discover its unique properties. Place it on the floor. Jump over it, put one part of you inside it, crawl in and under it. In groups create a narrative or situation that uses the boxes as if they are mountain-side caves, or as if one of the boxes contains a bomb – compose a movement sequence that captures the atmosphere of terror.

STICKS

Explore moving with a stick. What can you do with a stick? Create a movement sequence around the different ways of using a stick, for example as a tennis racquet, a golf club, a ski stick, a walking stick, an oar or a whip.

ENVIRONMENT AS A PROP

Use the environment as a prop.

Explore the location, the shapes and relationships suggested by the location, such as a staircase, a picnic table, a doorway, a playground. Find ways of moving in the environment and as a result of the environment that expresses its uniqueness.

Stories

NON-VERBAL STORIES

Walk across the space, stop, turn and walk back. Walk across, hesitate, look over your shoulder, and run the rest of the way. Find different ways of crossing, using only walking, stopping and turning. Let your body tell a story.

Movement sequence using sticks

STORY-TELLING

One person improvises the telling of a story such as 'The Three Little Pigs'. The others perform the story, either reacting to the rhythm of the words or depicting the story in movement.

Try the same with an existing story such as an African folktale or 'The Owl and the Pussy Cat', or make up original stories. Tell stories around a theme such as 'Metamorphoses – Birth to Death'. Story telling through movement needs to become less gestural as pupils get older.

Activities

SPORTS DAY

Begin by identifying the types of movements that happen during sports day:

running	dodging	crouching
turning	darting	falling
jumping	hitting	walking
clapping	sprinting	throwing
catching	leaping	hurdles
transference of weight		

Practise these at normal and exaggerated size and at different speeds.

Practise running and stopping and freezing in shapes that one sees at a Sports Day meeting. Make the shapes clear, and emphasise sudden stops and quick direction changes. Create a movement phrase from some of the words above and create an ending that looks like a photograph for a newspaper headline. Do the movement phrases altogether in slow motion and end in a group photo.

SPORT ACTIVITIES

Play with an imaginary tennis ball. Throw it, kick it, bounce it, roll it. Now imagine that it is a large light beach ball. Play with a googly ball (one with weights inside that tends to go off at a tangent). Throw your imaginary ball to someone else. Have a throw-and-catch game with your partner.

Choose a sport that you like such as tennis, golf or football. Choose one basic movement from that sport and practise that movement.

Think about its beginning and ending. Let the ending lead to the beginning so that it becomes continuous. Identify the climax of the movement. Get into a rhythm with the movement.

Exaggerate it. Begin to play with the rhythm, do it slow motion and double time, then reverse the movement as if rewinding a movie. Syncopate the movement by delaying or speeding up parts of the movement. Allow the movement to become abstracted.

OBSTACLE RACE

Create a movement phrase from these words in any order:

jump	leap	fall	roll
stretch	bend	twist	

Set up an obstacle course using props and move through the course a number of times, using your movement phrase. Be aware of the rhythm that is created. Remove the props and, maintaining the rhythm, perform the movement phrase.

WORK TASKS

Explore work tasks in movement:
- washing the windows
- decorating the room
- picking the apples
- painting the house
- chopping the wood
- mowing the lawn

Let the movements be rhythmic and exaggerated. Play with the movements in slow motion at double speed and syncopated. In groups of five, find a rhythmic chain gang type of movement, for instance on a farm picking, sorting, packing and sending apples, or in a bottling factory washing, rinsing, filling, capping, labelling and packing. Emphasise the rhythm and play with syncopation, slow motion and sudden freezes.

Ideas

SPACESHIP

Move as if you have just arrived in a spaceship and you have never seen 'earth things' before. Relate to them any way you like. Explore them, using all your senses and see what you can do with them.

SENSES, TEXTURES

Find ways to explore your different senses – hearing, feeling, touching, tasting. Move about the space and feel the different textures. Try to express those textures in movement.

CHANGING THE FLAVOUR

In groups of four, one person makes a movement phrase and then freezes.

The next person repeats the movement exactly and adds a new phrase and then freezes. The third person copies the last phrase of the previous person and adds on a new phrase.

Continue this way around the group. Add a Western (cowboys and so on), an Eastern, a comic or a tragic flavour.

MACHINES

Think about the movements of the parts of a sewing machine. Use different parts of your body to move like different parts of the machine.
Ask what other machines pupils have seen – clocks, computers, toasters and so on. Ask about the moving parts and how they relate to one another.
Explore the mechanical type of movement and sound made by a vacuum cleaner or a car.

Using each part of your body as a part of the machine, create your own imaginary 'super-machine'. Add the sounds your machine would make.

What is a typical machine-type movement? Machines are a characteristic of modernity and industrialisation. How is the machine type movement reflected in modern dance and music?

In groups of five, create one machine using five bodies. Each part of the machine makes a sound. Vary the action by adding freezes, slow motion, double speed, syncopation.

Write down 20 words that describe how you feel about your country at this moment. Do not write your name on your list.

Place all the lists in a pile in the centre of the room. Each student take a list, making sure it is not your own. Very quickly, go round the circle and each person read out the words on the list you hold.

Choose any word that strikes you from those that you have heard. Compose a movement and a sound that expresses that word. Repeat with two more words. Join your movements together.

In twos, teach one another your sound and movement phrases and join them together. Then join another couple and once again teach one another your extended movement and sound sequences. Make sure you have a strong beginning and ending. Keep making the group larger by joining other groups as long as there is time available.

Discuss whether the dance is a reflection of your country at that particular time and whether or how the art of Dance can be a mirror to society.

Emotions

'Motion arouses emotion, and emotion also brings forth motion, and the moment we speak of emotion communication is involved.' (*Louis Horst*)

Feeling tone can be introduced when the words used to stimulate a movement conjure up a memory of feelings: struggle, listen, scream. This may encourage an awareness of how emotion is expressed through the body and provide an opportunity for pupils to release pent-up feelings in a safe environment.

One can explore how mood affects movement, how movement affects mood and how the body reflects the mood. Eliciting emotive expression is difficult and students often respond with stereotypical interpretations. These responses can be used as a starting point for encouraging students to recognise and challenge stereo-typing.

FEELINGS

Sit facing the back of the room, eyes closed. Using your back only, allow it to portray:

agitation	anger	depression
sadness	ecstasy	expectancy
concern	peacefulness	

Then explore some of these emotions in different ways. For example use only your hands (or torso, face, lower body and so on).

Facing a partner, using the face only, one person portrays an emotion and the other copies it as exactly as possible. Each takes a turn to lead.

Then one partner expresses a feeling and the other partner reacts in movement to the feelings.

fear	sorrow	contentment
wonder	shame	hope
loneliness	anxiety	reverence
hate	rage	repentance
boredom	pain	satisfaction
horror	love	resignation
frustration	joy	jealousy
pride	despair	resentment

This activity focuses attention on feeling, rather than on seeing the movement.

Sit in a comfortable position with your eyes closed. As words are called out, try to remember a time when you or someone you know felt that feeling. Try to express through your body what that felt like.

Choose a shape that portrays surprise, fear, and then sadness. Add movement between the shapes, vary the level and pay attention to your focus. Repeat the exercise choosing your own three words. In twos, perform your sequence for your partner and see if s/he can identify the emotions you selected.

MOOD

Make a movement phrase that the whole class learns. In groups of six, each group uses the same movement phrase to depict a different mood or atmosphere.

Extreme boredom

Violence

In a society in need of healing and transformation, dealing with the issue of violence in a safe environment can be very cathartic. Pupils can confront their feelings and fears and role-play their anger.

The exercise on fighting and falling can be very beneficial but must be very carefully handled. Only use it with older pupils who have a certain amount of self-control, and only when an atmosphere of trust and control has been established in the class.

Make sure that pupils learn how to fall safely first. Teach the pupils to get very close to the floor before they fall. A fall is never really a fall but a place – place yourself as close to the floor as you can and then simulate falling and sliding. Always fall on flat bones and well padded places such as thighs or shoulders. Never fall on a hand, elbow or any other pointy bone. Practise falling in all directions. When you fall and roll, curve and soften the spine.

FIGHTS AND FALLS

Move around the space punching as hard as you can. Be sure not to touch anyone else or anything. Punch forwards, backwards and sidewards. Think of someone you are angry with, whom you would really like to punch. Punch at a wall in the room, but control your fist just before impact. Practise this many times.

Now kick in every direction. Punch and kick – use every bit of energy and anger you can muster. Add sounds to your effort.

Imagine that you are being punched and kicked. How will your body react? Punch and kick an imaginary enemy, and defend yourself when you get punched. How does it feel to be kicked under the chin, in your stomach, behind your knees?

Now you are being punched so hard you fall to the floor. Scramble up and be kicked and punched again. Try an imaginary fight with strong aggressive movements but avoiding hitting and punching gestures.

Find a partner. The rule is: no-one may touch his/her partner. Working in slow motion, practise kicking and punching your partner without touching them. As one partner punches or kicks, the other receives, falls or defends. Be careful not to hit at the same time. Work out a fight that will look real. Continue to work in slow motion.

Work out who you are (a character role) and what the fight is about. Practise until you are certain of the moves. Add sounds. Watch one another.

Discuss the issue of violence and then take this into activities in other areas of the curriculum, for instance write a poem about violence, a story, or a play, or discuss how fighting and violence have shaped history, national boundaries and economics.

CHAPTER 13

Sound and movement

Body movement creates sound; think of the sound of breathing and the sound of the feet on the ground. Whether or not it can be heard, there is a sound inherent in every movement we make, and movement inherent in every sound we make. At their point of origin, within us, the art of movement-dance, and the art of sound-music, are one. Developing the ability to express ourselves simultaneously in movement and sound can facilitate a dynamic expressivity. For example a person who talks without moving her/his body, uses the body in monotone, and is more likely to be boring than a person who is animated and uses the body to add energy and emphasis to their speech.

Pupils can explore combining sound and movement, and experience the feeling of the sound and movement coming from the same impulse.

Rhythmic patterns on the floor

HANDS AND FEET

Explore the sounds you can make with your hands such as clapping, brushing, clicking, banging, scraping, slapping the floor or your own body or any object to make an accompaniment for yourself as you dance. Make as much sound as you can – let this be a very noisy dance.

Walk and listen to the sound of your feet on the floor. Intensify the sound by stamping slightly. Explore sounds made by the feet such as brushing, scraping, and shuffling. Make different patterns of sound with your feet.

Now make as much sound as you can with your hands and feet. Now dance, accompanying yourself with your hands and feet.

In pairs, one makes the sounds while the other dances.

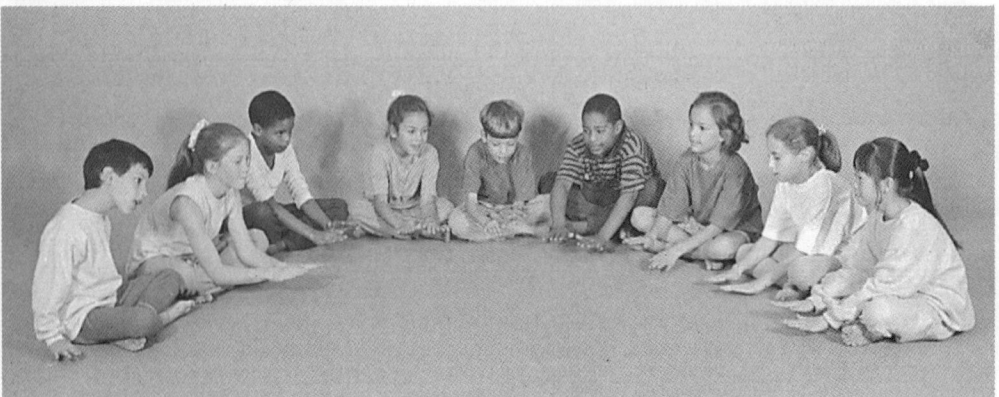

PERSONAL RESOURCES

Create an interesting sound pattern by clapping your hands together ... slapping your hands against your thighs ... snapping your fingers ... striking different parts of your body or different objects ... using various parts of the body in contact with each other. Use all your personal resources and any objects in the room as instruments – voice, hands and feet, floor, walls – to accompany yourself in sound while improvising freely in movement.

INSTRUMENTS

Use home-made or percussion instruments. Choose an instrument to play and bring out its unique quality. Be aware of the movement you must make to produce the sound. Exaggerate it. Make it with your whole body. Unite yourself with your instrument through movement. Let the instrument become part of you. Find a movement that takes you across the floor, and that feels right with your sound. Form a procession with one person leading and setting up a rhythm and everyone else joining in.

Moving to a group orchestra

UNISON

As a group, form a circle or line. One person after another takes a turn in the centre of the circle (or in front of the line) creating a pattern of sound and movement which s/he repeats over and over again. The whole group joins in doing the same thing at the same time. Each leader should try to create a pattern as different as possible from the preceding one.

ALTERNATING

As above except the leader and the group alternate. The leader executes the pattern only once and waits while the group repeats it. Then the group waits while the leader repeats the pattern and so on.

UNISON LOCOMOTOR

As for 'Unison' above except that the movement is locomotor. The leader, followed by the entire group, proceeds from one end of the room to the other, all repeating the leader's sound and movement pattern simultaneously.

Then the leader goes to the back of the line and the next in line becomes leader.

Voice and movement

The following exercises may sometimes come as a shock to students who are unprepared for this type of experience, and may be met with resistance. As the teacher you need to take a strong position and not allow the students to retreat. Rather challenge them boldly to courageous action. Tell them that this is an opportunity to go beyond their comfort zones and to be 'silly' in a safe environment. These exercises are for students who have been doing Creative Dance for a while, where a group trust has been established, otherwise people become self-conscious and the exercise will not work.

MOVEMENT QUALITIES WITH VOICE

Lie on the floor with eyes closed. Breathe in and whoosh the air out. Breathe in and let the air out with a sssss. Breathe in and breathe out loudly. With every breath out allow the body to move. Yawn with your voice and body. Sigh with voice and body.

Explore the feeling of the following words in sound and movement. Let your voice and body work together.

tight	prickly	bubbly	rough
closed	heavy	small	slow
smooth	slippery	squeaky	lose
contracting	light	curved	fast
strong	rubbery	muddy	hard
expanding	regular	straight	flat
weak	silky	oily	soft
round	high	irregular	rising
animal-like	sudden	scratchy	bumpy
sinking	open	low	large
gradual	insect-like		

Unison locomotor with sound

FAMILIAR SOUNDS WITH MOVEMENT

Now explore some sounds with your voice and your whole body as vividly as you can. Express the quality of the sound rather than acting out the sound.

grunting	hissing	sobbing
whispering	clicking	popping
whining	spluttering	squeaking
growling	humming	shouting
laughing	whistling	groaning
sneezing	mumbling	croaking

Sometimes students become so absorbed in making the sounds that they forget the movement aspect of the exercise. To counteract this tendency, ask them occasionally to express the quality of the sound silently through movement alone.

KNOWN LANGUAGE

Make a single movement, accompanying it with a single known word in any language of your choice. Let the word be an outgrowth of the movement.

Experiment with movement and words in different ways: make a single movement with a series of words of a phrase … improvise freely, accompanying yourself with spoken words … tell a story in movement and words … create a poem in movement and words.

SOUND EXTRACTS

Take one group of words, soft sounding words, for instance, as the source of the dance. Do not use the words as words – rather use the sounds suggested by the words to create a group dance.

105

SPEECH SOUNDS

Explore the movement feeling of each of these vowel sounds by improvising freely in movement while speaking the sound. Try speaking the sound in different ways:

ah   oh   ee   oo   ow   ai   uh

In the same way explore the movement feeling of these consonant sounds:

b   f   g   h   j   k   l   m   p   r
s   t   v   z

Put consonants and vowels together: b-ee; p-ah; s-ooh. Put syllables together into 'mumbo-jumbo' words. Tell a story in movement and words using your own language.

Working in twos have a conversation in sound and movement, each speaking your own language – be sure that you do not both 'speak' at the same time. Let one partner tell a mumbo-jumbo story while the other expresses the story in movement, adjusting the movement to the words.

Try out other mumbo-jumbo ideas. For example, one person is the orator, making a speech and everyone else is the audience reacting to the sounds; or you are at a cocktail party conversing in mumbo-jumbo sound and movement.

These exercises work very well where there is a language barrier and students come to realise that they can communicate even when they don't speak the same language.

SOUND QUALITY

The sounds of words do not only have specific meaning and emotional connotations but can also have different qualities of sound.

- soft sounding words …   whispering
- round sounding words … moon
- slow sounding words … dreamily
- quick sounding words … pinprick
- hard sounding words … cracking
- thin sounding words … slip

Sound can be extracted from words and used to accompany movement. The sound of whispering, for example, produces a long hissing sound, evoking a long slithery movement; a short word like 'peep' would evoke a short, sharp movement.

POETRY IN SOUND AND MOVEMENT

Certain poems lend themselves well to sound and movement interpretation. For instance poems such as 'Jabberwocky' by Lewis Carroll, and Edward Lear's 'The Quangle-Wangle's Hat' coined mumbo-jumbo words that are very evocative. Choose or write a poem. Experiment with movements that express the words and then work out a presentation of the poem, alone or in groups, in sound and movement. Alternatively, working in groups, some say the poem as others perform it.

CHAPTER 14
Group work

Fostering the ability to interact positively with other people, to share, co-operate and work together, is perhaps one of the most important tasks of an effective education system. The ability to not only tolerate one another, but to be able to negotiate our differences, is a skill that needs our utmost attention.

Through Creative Dance, in an environment which accepts and welcomes diversity, participants have an opportunity to build skills that facilitate decision-making and problem-solving together. Students learn to negotiate the communal use of power, of space and of time. They become aware of cultural commonalities and differences, and find ways to combine or fuse cultural preferences or to promote their own cultural expression. The non-verbal nature of dance paves the way for experiences in socialisation that are not limited by language.

Dancing in a group requires inter-sensitivity and physical contact. It takes time to build the trust that allows this. Regular opportunities need to be provided to develop trust of oneself and others within a group. For a group to function as a unit, individuals need to learn to merge and submerge, to submit to a larger vision.

Creative Dance is a leveller. The nature of the subject emphasises each person's uniqueness and therefore promotes non-competitiveness. The process and the experience in the moment are more important than previous background and training or than any particular product or performance.

TRUST CIRCLE

In groups of about eight participants, one person stands in the centre with eyes closed. The others form a circle around him/her and gently pat, pinch and pummel the centre person all over his/her body (being careful not to embarrass the person by touching private parts). The centre person, staying rooted on one spot with feet together, keeping their body straight and inflexible, begins to tilt off-balance in one direction. The members of the group catch, support and gently push him/her back towards the centre at which point s/he falls in another direction. Finally the person is lifted by the whole group horizontally as high as the group can reach and then lowered slowly and gently to the floor. Each person in the group has a turn at being the centre person.

BLIND AND GUIDE

Begin with everyone lying down, relaxing, eyes closed. Select half the class by touching them lightly and inviting them to leave the room silently. The others remain lying down with their eyes closed. The group outside are instructed to return quietly to the room and select one lying-down person – not their closest friend.

Supporting the partner, whose eyes must remain closed throughout, the guide, A, places one arm firmly around B, the blind partner's waist and with the other hand, holds B's hand out in front of them. A then takes B on a tactile walk, outside if possible, touching all kinds of different surfaces – leaves, floor, sand, carpet, wall, another person's hair. A takes care of B and ensure that B is absolutely safe. B should not know who is taking care of him/her. A must not talk or laugh or let B hear his/her voice. After about 10 minutes, A returns B to the floor and goes and sits far away. *Repeat the whole process with the B group guiding the A group. On completion of the exercise the groups discuss their experience and individuals find out who their guides were.*

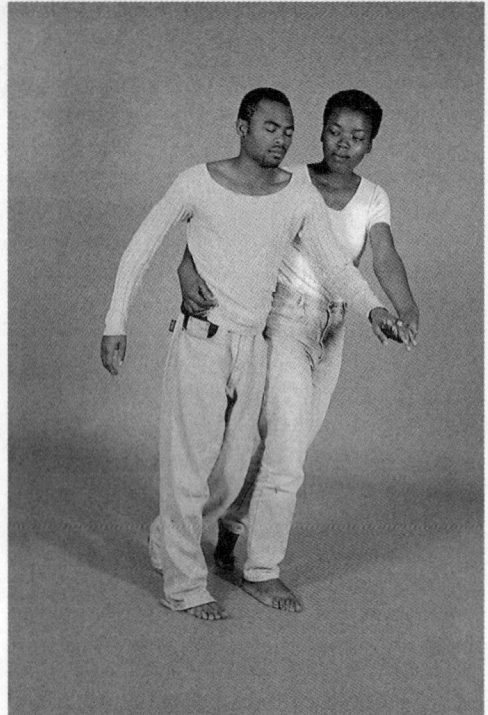

Blind and guide

MULTIBODY CREATURE

In groups of three or four, experiment with ways of creating one creature.

Participants become attached in different ways. Keep an awareness of the whole creature. Some parts of one of the bodies can be hidden; use surprises and play with optical illusions.

CREATING A CHAIR

Two people together create a chair with their bodies for a third to sit on, lie in, rock on or be carried in.

THE 'OTHER'

In a group of six, five people move to the same rhythm and pattern formation while the sixth moves to a different rhythm. The group must find a way of incorporating the sixth person.

GROUP SCULPTURE

One large group, A, forms a group sculpture without the other group, B, watching. B then looks at the sculpture and copies it as exactly and as quickly as possible.

MIRROR IMAGING

In twos, partners sitting facing each other. Begin with hands only. A leads by moving her/his hands slowly and smoothly and B copies the movements exactly. The movements should be so simultaneous that an outsider watching should not be able to tell who is leading. Try to maintain easy eye contact throughout, without staring.

Before changing over to B leading, partners discuss whether they were able to maintain eye contact, and how it felt. Note that in some cultures, it is not usual to make eye contact and this exercise may therefore be more difficult for some people.

Begin to use different parts of the body, progress to using the whole body, and to moving across the floor, alternating leadership. After much practice, allow the leadership to pass back and forth (without any verbal contact). Try mirror exercises in threes, and in large groups. Try standing across the room from a partner, with movement mirrored from afar.

Delay using this exercise until students have some movement vocabulary or it becomes very static.

Bottom left and above: Mirror imaging

GROUP SWAY

The group stands in a large circle, facing inwards, with shoulders and backs of hands connecting and eyes closed.

Allow a natural sway to develop – do not manipulate the movement. Once it has begun, allow it to grow larger until the group is swaying from one foot to the other, as far as it can go. Once the sway has reached its peak, allow it to die down and stop in its own time.

AMOEBA

Let the whole class stand in a tight group with everyone attached in some way.
Allow the group to begin to move as a whole very slowly and smoothly across the space, with everyone constantly remaining in contact. Everyone must keep moving all the time. At the other end of the room, freeze as a group and become aware of the design that has been created.

GROUP UNISON

There is a special pleasure in moving in unison with others, perhaps because it engenders a feeling of agreement and support – or anonymity.

The group begins in a cluster in the space, all facing in the same direction. The dancer who seems to be at the head of the group begins to move slowly and simply, keeping in mind that others are following.

The others move in unison with this dancer. As the facing of the movement (and therefore the group) changes, so does the leadership. It is always the person who can not see the others who automatically becomes the leader. When more than one person is at the front, smoothly without speaking allow one person to become dominant. Aim to have a smooth transition from one leader to another, interrupting the movement flow as little as possible.

UNISON MOVEMENT

Use two groups simultaneously, each with its own leader.
The leaders move as they wish, and the followers may imitate either leader, from near or far. They may change from one to the other at their own discretion but should maintain an unbroken performance presence through the transitions. The leaders determine not only the movement, but the relationship between the groups, contrasting speed, level and shape, perhaps keeping stationary for a while or creating a dialogue between the two groups. The followers determine the visual interest and should change frequently.

ETERNAL TRIANGLE

In groups of three, two of the dancers work as a duet establishing a repetitive movement theme. The third dancer tries to force, tease or seduce one of them away. Let the dance find its own resolution.

PARTNER RELAXATION

Sit in twos, both facing the same way. The person behind, A, using cupped hands, pats the front person's back B. Follow this with a strong massage of B's shoulders, with A's hands working up through B's hair. A, sitting closely behind and supporting B's body, rocks B from side to side. Reverse the exercise, with B relaxing A.

Moving in unison

COFFIN PASS

As a class, or in large groups, form two parallel lines, two to three feet apart, facing each other, making a 'people hallway'. One person stands at the end of the people hallway with his/her back to them and starts to lean back as though lying down. Immediately, the nearest people in both lines take the weight of the head, neck, torso and begin to pass him/her head first down the hallway, supporting the various parts of the body as s/he gets passed along. At the end of the hallway s/he is put down and the next person in line is passed along, until everyone has had a chance.

MOVEMENT WHISPERS

The group stands in a circle, with eyes closed. The first person opens their eyes and makes a short movement phrase, while the person alongside watches. The first person repeats the movement phrase exactly once again.

The person watching then performs the exact same phrase while the third person opens their eyes to watch. The movement phrase is passed around the whole group in this way until it finally returns to the first person who checks to see whether the original movement phrase has remained the same or changed drastically with the numerous interpretations.

EQUIPOISE

In twos, face each other, holding each other's wrists, with toes touching, and lean back, keeping the body straight and rigid. After finding your balance and returning evenly to an upright, positiion try leans and balances in other positions: facing the same way, holding hands (A's left and B's right hand) and feet alongside of one another. When in balance, allow your outside arms to be raised without interfering with the balance. Try also to raise one leg each, without affecting the balance. Another alternative is for the two partners to face opposite ways and both use the same hand. For example, both using the left, join hands and lean away. Facing one another, but standing about an arm's length apart, place open hands, palms outwards in front of your chest. Fall towards each other, catching each other with the outward turned hands.

As you fall make a spontaneous sound. As you push one another away simultaneously, utter your partner's sound.

CONSTRUCTING A DANCE

In groups of three to five participants, begin with one person creating a short movement phrase, which the group watches and copies. Each person, in turn, adds on to the original phrase until a dance is created using and combining all the contributions. Take this further by deciding, as a group, how to vary the phrases, change direction, reverse sequences, add repetition, stillness and variations in time, space and force. This can be done with much larger groups as well.

GIVING AND RECEIVING WEIGHT

In pairs, one person gives his/her weight to the other who gives support. Smoothly transfer the weight the other way, and then keep passing the weight back and forth. Choose four or five different positions of support and keep practising them. Develop the transitions between the positions. Make sure the weight flows easily back and forth.

BODY LANGUAGE

Watch your partner as he/she talks. Introduce a variety of different subjects, including some that may be joyous, controversial or threatening.

See if you can detect his/her mood, how s/he holds him/herself, shifts weight. Begin to watch how other people use their bodies to express themselves. Walk behind different strangers in the street and without drawing attention to yourself or antagonising anyone, try to copy different ways that people walk. From people's walks, see if you can discern something about them: how do they feel about themselves? Are they confident, self-conscious, depressed?

Demonstrate to the class one of these walks and develop a character sketch of the person.

Giving and receiving weight

THE HUDDLE

Six or seven people stand very close together facing one another. They form a huddle by bending forwards, knees a little bent, arms around each other's shoulders and waists, meshing as a strong structure. One person detaches and begins to climb up the outside of the huddle, perhaps placing a foot on someone's thigh, a hand in the crook of someone's neck and another hand on someone's arm.

Moving across the top of the huddle, and down the other side, the person remains closely identified with the mass and resumes a place in the huddle. Immediately, someone else takes the decision to be next to climb.

Depending on the strength and cohesiveness of the group, more than one person may climb at the same time.

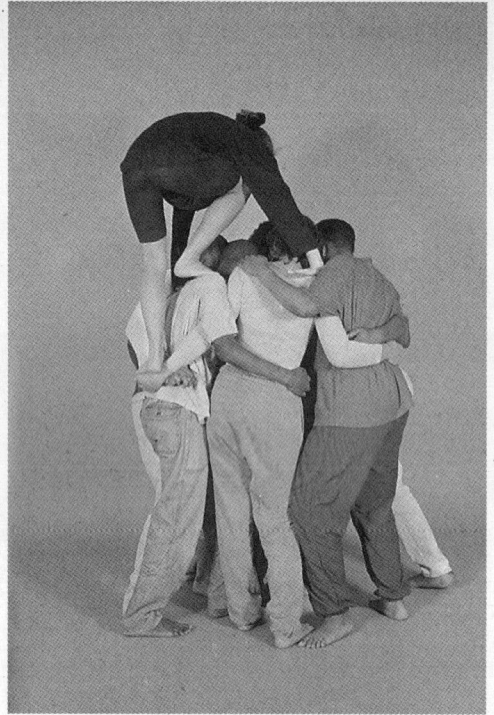

A huddle in progress

CHAPTER 15

Dancing across the curriculum

Two basic concepts underpin the approach in this chapter. The first is that the fragmentation and compartmentalisation of subjects in schools makes it difficult for pupils to make connections between them, or to relate their learning to the real world. A compartmentalised world-view results, especially with examination-oriented teaching. It creates tunnel vision and prevents creative, holistic, integrated learning. Integrating dance with other subjects helps pupils to see how different aspects of knowing are connected. They can learn how ideas from one field permeate and influence ideas and activities in others.

The second concept is the belief that people learn more effectively when they learn experientially. Because movement is fundamental to life, it connects with a great deal of what is learnt. Opportunities can be provided through dance to experience concepts vibrantly, and in different ways. In Science, for example, experiencing the concept of weight can make ideas on matter and gravity easier to understand.

Learning occurs through the senses. Knowledge is acquired through sight (seeing, reading), hearing (listening, talking) and through feel and touch. Movement is a motor experience, sensed through the muscles (kinesthetic sense), independent of ear and eye. It is possible to have a dance experience without hearing or sight. Nevertheless the complete dance experience involves all the senses, with the kinesthetic sense co-ordinating. The kinesthetic sense is the most inner of all our senses, informing us of occurrences within our own body. Lessons can be constructed that begin by focusing on pure movement, increasingly involve sound and/or sight; or they may begin with sight or sound and progress to movement.

The following ideas are only some of the ways that dance can be integrated with other subjects. It is hoped that these ideas will stimulate teachers to find many further innovative ways to work across the curriculum.

Dance and Art

LIGHT AND COLOUR

Improvise freely on each of these themes: light, darkness, red, violet. Discuss what kinds of movements these images evoke.

Choose one colour and create a dance that gives expression to the atmosphere evoked by that colour. Examples might be 'Red the Dangerous', 'Green the Life-giver' or 'Violet the Passive'. Using any old clothes, scraps of material, newspaper and paint, create an impromptu costume for your dance.

VISUAL PATTERNING

Look around you for something that has an interesting visual pattern: a tree, a chair. Look at it carefully, study its shape, lines, planes, volume, mass, texture and colour. Sense the qualities of its unique design through your whole body. Now express it in movement.

MOVEMENT TO SCULPTURE

Make a movement with a clear and interesting visual design. Recreate the design of the movement in some material or combination of materials (wire, string, paper, glass, wood, clay), choosing your materials carefully to bring out the design.

SCULPTURE TO MOVEMENT

Make a clay sculpture and then make a movement piece based on your sculpture and, later, a partner's sculpture. Let the shapes move.

ART GALLERY

Visit an art gallery. Choose one painting or sculpture that interests you. Look at the shapes, the colours, lines and atmosphere. Express the painting in movement terms.

COLLAGE

Explore the shapes and pathways of falling leaves in movement. Gather fallen leaves and make a collage.

MAGAZINES

Choose three pictures from magazines. Create a movement inspired by each picture. Join them together.

PHOTOGRAPHS

Select a group photograph before the session. As a group, look at your photograph and copy the static formation as closely as possible. Discuss what you think happened before and after the photograph. Choreograph a dramatic dance sequence that uses the static pose, the 'before' and 'after' scenarios in any order. These sequences can be recreated in the past, present or future.

The way drawing and movement are used in the next three exercises, is not intended to improve artistic ability or drawing skills. It provides an opportunity, rather, to realise that everyone can draw, dance, develop the imagination and learn something about oneself through these media.

Discourage pupils from being judgemental about their drawings, emphasise the process rather than the product. Large sheets of newsprint are most helpful so that the sensation of movement can be retained when drawing.

SIGNATURE DANCE

Use large sheets of newsprint and flat crayons. Write your signature all over the page. Try writing with either hand, both hands, toes, mouth. Let your whole body participate in the writing of your signature ... write your signature in the air with your finger ... write it larger with your hand ... dance your signature with your whole body.

SOUND MOVEMENT CONVERSION

Divide a large sheet of paper into three sections. Listen to three different pieces of music and, using one section of your paper for each piece of music, draw patterns freely as you listen. Turn off the music and convert your three patterns into movement patterns. Put on the music again and dance your patterns.

SELF-PORTRAIT

A self-portrait dance can be therapeutic because it provides an opportunity to learn something about oneself while expressing one's feelings.

On newsprint, using fat crayons, quickly draw a graphic representation of how you see yourself. Use one word to describe your drawing and make that the title of the drawing. Now compose a movement or series of movements that expresses that word.

On a second piece of newsprint quickly draw how you think others see you. Choose a word to describe your drawing, compose a movement expression and join it to your previous movement(s).

On a third piece of paper, draw where you are heading or how you wish to be. Name it, compose it and use the movements to complete your self-portrait dance.

THE ELEMENTS

Begin with pupils lying face down in a circle with all heads facing centre, forehead on arms. Use gentle atmospheric music such as whale music, water music.

Think about how a tiny tadpole moves with just a head and a tail. Begin to move your head in a figure eight motion like a tadpole … let your shoulders become involved … allow your upper torso to become involved in the movement. Now begin to move that part of your body where a tail would be attached if you had one, swishing it from side to side. Begin to focus on movements of the arms and legs … feel them, move them … experiment with pushing away from the surface. Now become aware of the power of your legs … as if moving through water and finally on to land and hopping into the air.

On your piece of newsprint, draw large movements. Don't plan your drawing … allow it to happen. Don't be separate from the drawing … involve your whole body and allow your voice to be part of the drawing. Don't judge the drawing … draw for the sake of drawing, not to design a picture … keep filling your page.

Distance yourself from your drawing, look at it and write on it the first word that comes into your mind.

Pupils can be taken through this process a number of times, exploring the different elements – earth, air (wind), fire, water.

● a grain of sand in a desert … rolling, moving in the wind, gathering together and dispersing, shaping and reshaping the landscape. Moving softly bumping up against one another and gathering momentum, moving strongly as a force together. Discuss the feeling of one grain of sand blowing and sand stinging as many grains blow together.

• *fire* ... a tiny tentative flicker, growing into a flaming blaze with fireballs leaping across space, devouring all in its path and dying down to ashes. At each stage, students express the mood or essence on paper.
• *wind/air* ... spinning around and running forward and backward to feel the wind on your arms.
At the end of the class arrange all the drawings on the floor as an exhibition and encourage students to notice the kinds of thoughts and feelings that have emerged.

Dance and Mathematics

Dance can aid the teaching of mathematical concepts. Mathematics is basically the study of quantitative relationships, so dance activities concerned with relationships of time (as in rhythm) and space are supportive of Mathematics.

POLY-RHYTHMS AND DIVISION

Count aloud to six rhythmically and repeatedly. Accent with a clap on the first beat of six. Break the six beats into two halves and accent the beginning of both halves (on one and on four). How many counts in each half? (3).

Do the same with breaking six beats into three equal parts. One group beats the 12 34 56 while the other beats 123 456. Practise separately and then do together for syncopation.

Elicit that 6 divided by 2 = 3 and 6 divided by 3 = 2.

OPPOSITE POLES

Experiment with the meaning of opposite poles frequently used in Mathematics, such as
• more than <, less than >;
• greater than, smaller than;
• higher, lower;
• plus, minus;
• multiply, divide.

GEOMETRY

Explore a soft curved, rounded movement, close to you and far from you. What does it feel like?
What are the characteristics of a circle?
See how many ways you can use your body to make a straight line, horizontal, vertical, diagonal. How do linear movements make you feel? How are they different from circular movements? What are the characteristics of a line? What angles do you possess within your own body? Explore the angularity of knee and elbow movements. How are angular movements different from circles and lines? In groups of four, use your bodies to create a square, rectangle, hexagon, octagon and pentagon.

ELASTIC GEOMETRY

Use elastic sewn into loops to explore equilateral and isosceles triangles, squares, rhombus, acute, right and obtuse angles. Once the class know exactly what these are, each student composes a dance that moves through five geometric shapes, pausing in each shape long enough for the rest of the class to identify them.

MEASUREMENT AND COUNTING

Use your body to measure the space or objects in the space. For instance, measure how many footsteps from wall to wall. How many body lengths across the width and length of the space? How many steps does it takes to run around the circumference of the room?

Dance and Language

WORDS INTO SHAPES INTO WORDS

Make words out of body shapes: What word describes that shape? What does it remind you of? Find a word to describe that shape.

Make body shapes out of words such as twisted, gross, flat, jagged.

PARTS OF SPEECH

Write a list of body parts on the board or on newsprint on the wall, or on cards. Title these *nouns*. Write lists of action words, headed *verbs*. Divide the class into small groups of three or four. The class leader secretly tells each group to move in a certain way.

The class describes how they see a group moving, and these words are written up as *adjectives*. Each group chooses one word from each list (a noun, a verb and an adjective) and compose a movement sentence using the three words.

How you present this will depend on the age and the group's previous exposure to parts of speech.

CLICHÉS

Explore some of the following clichés individually. In groups choose a cliché, and decide on a way to structure it into an improvisation. Let the rest of the class try to guess what the cliché, is.
- armed to the teeth
- down and out
- in full swing
- make ends meet
- neither here nor there
- pull one's weight
- put one's foot down
- take it or leave it
- haven't a leg to stand on
- at one fell swoop
- hold one's own
- hanging in the balance
- play fast and loose
- lose one's grip
- done to a turn
- straight from the shoulder
- throw someone over

POETRY

Read a poem. Let the pupils improvise just to the rhythm and intonation of the poem. Explore the movement words. Improvise to the poem line by line. In groups, let one person read the poem while the others perform it.

SEA POEM

Explore the movements of the sea: a wave breaking, crashing, rolling, sucking back into the sea; the creatures in the sea, the fish, seaweed, crabs and sand. Write a poem about the sea.

Dance and Drama

Generally, the material of dance is movement, and the material of drama is verbal language and action. However, dance and drama overlap in many ways. The boundaries between the two art forms permeable and new forms such as 'Physical Theatre' have emerged. Both art forms use the same instrument: the human body.

Many of the exercises in this book incorporate both dance and drama. Here are a few more.

Dance and Science

Dance and Geography

CHAPTER 16

Cultural Studies

Creative Dance is based on principles of human movement which are essentially universal. Creative Dance is not limited to any particular style, period, vocabulary, historical or social context, nor is it a prescribed set of steps or a language. Creative Dance celebrates the uniqueness of the individual while affirming the commonality of the human and natural elements inherent in each of us.

Artistic choices, interpretations and social interactions in dance are, however, influenced by a person's culture or way of 'doing things'. Any choreographic work reflects the dance-artist's sense of identity, social values and psychological perspectives. In a poly-cultural society, students working together from different cultural backgrounds may facilitate a mixing of different dance forms. New and interesting outcomes may emerge, generating an enhanced dance vocabulary and a richness of meaning. The more cultural influences are allowed to permeate the dance experience, the more accurately it will reflect our poly-cultural society.

The study of dance as part of cultural education gives students insight into their own heritage as well as that of others, to understand how dance is influenced by, and influences, culture. The more opportunities provided for people of all cultural backgrounds to feel accepted and appreciated, the more likely they are to develop their potential. Creative Dance also contributes to aesthetic education as students learn to appreciate dance as a form of art. The learners should be encouraged to respond to dance in a personal way. They should have opportunities to think about, describe, discuss and analyse their dance experiences. The ultimate aim is to create an awareness of the importance of expressive movement in everyday life. In addition, learners should have an opportunity to develop an appreciation of dance as a performing art.

Wherever possible, students should be stimulated by open-ended discussions, drawing, painting and writing. Appropriate magazines, books and audio-visual material should be available for reference. To facilitate discussion, outings to see live performances should be arranged and learners encouraged to watch and discuss dance programmes on television Pictures, drawings and writing about dance can be collected in a workbook or journal.

To help children to develop an understanding and awareness of the way dance is made and how it is used for a range of purposes, learners should be encouraged to reflect about their own dancing, community dance, social and cultural aspects of dance and dance as a performing art.

Adapt the suggestions listed below to suit the particular age group. They range from very simple ideas for younger students to increasingly complex studies and research projects for mature students.

OWN DANCING

- Talk about why you and your peers dance?
- Discuss the different kinds of dancing you have done, how you feel when you are dancing and how it feels to make your own movements.
- What influences the type of dances you like? Discuss family, friends, culture, place, mode of upbringing and pressure to conform.

COMMUNITY DANCE

- What dances have you seen in your community?
- Where and when do people in your community dance?
- Describe the range of dance styles in your community and discuss why people do different styles of dance.

SOCIAL ASPECTS OF DANCE

- Use these topics and questions for class discussions
- Why do people dance? How is dance used for a range of purposes?
- Has dance been a reflection of society through the different ages?
- Ask your parents and grandparents to describe dances they have seen and done, and compare them with dances of today.
- Discuss various contemporary dance trends. What do they tell us about society in the 20th century?
- Examine two 20th century dances – for example one from the 1950s and one from the 1980s – and discuss how these dances fit into their periods.
- Identify similarities and differences in styles and eras of social, concert or ethnic dance.

- Read about the major cultural periods and the dominant styles of dance in different countries.
- Discuss how social cultural and historical context influence the nature of dance and the form and selection of movements.
- Identify and examine themes communicated through dance in different periods of time or in different cultures, in relation to important issues of the time.
- Recognise and discuss gender differences in dance from different times and places.
- Discuss why certain dance styles are seen more often on television than others.
- Compare dance as expression with dance as communication.
- Research and report on the social role of dance.

CULTURAL ASPECTS OF DANCE

- Identify South African dances, discuss their origin and compare the types of dance steps.
- Identify dances from different cultures and countries, focusing on costumes, patterning and groupings.
- Discuss clues in the music, costumes, formations, use of energy, space and movements that may identify the origins of a dance.
- Watch two dances from distinct cultures and compare the content, form and selection of movements.

DANCE AS A PERFORMING ART

- Perform your dance for others in the class.
- Watch other pupils' dances with attention.
- Watch a dance, pick your favourite movements and give reasons.
- Draw, paint or write about your favourite part of a dance.
- Discuss shapes, lines, levels and movements seen in books and pictures.
- Watch a pair of other pupils move, talk about their main movements and try to imitate them.
- Discuss, choose and prepare costumes for a dance event attended by friends and parents.
- Explore the way groups work to develop and present dances in theatre and community spaces.
- Rehearse and present a whole class dance. Ask for, and discuss, audience reaction.
- Plan and rehearse a series of dances in spaces around the school.
- Design a dance programme, complete with a short synopsis of the dance, biographies of the dancers and the choreographer, accompaniment and acknowledgements.
- Discuss the different styles of performance dance.
- Compare dance as entertainment with dance as art.
- Discuss the transition from dance as creative expression to dance as performance.

Conclusion

We wish you much success in your endeavours and hope that you find this book useful. We would appreciate any feedback about the book, the exercises or your experiences, and would welcome any ideas you would like to share.

Please feel free to contact either of us at the following addresses.

Jennifer van Papendorp
10 Park Avene
Camps Bay
Cape Town, 8001
Tel/Fax (021) 438-9769

Sharon Friedman
18 Campground Road
Rosebank
Cape Town, 7700
Tel (021) 689-5036

References and further reading

The following books and documents have provided ideas and stimulation, although not all are referred to directly in the text. They are recommended for further reading.

Blom, L.A. & Chaplin, T.C. (1982) *The Intimate Act of Choreography*. Pittsburgh: University of Pittsburgh Press.

Boorman, J. (1969) *Creative Dance in the First Three Grades*. Don Mills, Ontario: Longmans Canada Ltd.

Brinson, P. (1991) *Dance as Education: Towards a National Dance Culture*. London: The Falmer Press.

Collins, C. (1969) *Practical Modern Educational Dance*. London: MacDonalds and Evans.

De Haan Freed, M. (1976) *A Time to Teach, A Time to Dance: A Creative Approach to Teaching Dance*. USA: Jalmar Press Inc.

Gawain, S. (1989) Listening to inner wisdom, in *Healers on Healing*. Ed. Carlson, R & Shield, B. London: Rider

Grey, V. & Percival, R. (1962) *Music, Movement & Mime for Children*. London: Oxford University Press.

Halprin, L. & Burns, J. (1974) *Taking Part: A Workshop Approach to Collective Creativity*. Cambridge, Massachusetts: The MIT Press.

Harrison, K. & Auty, J. (1991) *Dance Ideas for Teachers, Students and Children*. London: Hodder & Stoughton.

Harrison, K., Layton, J. & Morris, M. (1989) *Dance and Movement*. Warwickshire: Scholastic Publications Ltd.

Hawkins, A.M. (1964) *Creating Through Dance*. Englewood Cliffs, New Jersey: Prentice-Hall.

H'Doubler, M.N. (1940) *Dance: A Creative Art Experience*. London: The University of Wisconsin Press.

Horst, L. (1969) Consider the question of Communication, in **Van Ruyl, M.** *Anthology of Impulse: Annual of Contemporary Dance 1951 - 1966*. Brooklyn: Impulse Publications.

Joyce, M. (1980) *First Steps in Teaching Creative Movement to Children*. Mountain View, California: Mayfield Publishing Company.

Laban, R. (1988) *The Mastery of Movement*. London: MacDonald and Evans.

Mettler, M. (1960) *Materials of Dance as a creative art activity*. Tucson, Arizona: Mettler Studios.

Morgenroth, J. (1987) *Dance Improvisations*. Pittsburgh: University of Pittsburgh Press.

Musgrave Horner, A. (1970) *Movement, Voice and Speech.* London: Methuen & Co Ltd.

Nicolls, B. (1974) *Move* . Richmond, Australia: Heinemann Educational Australia.

Preston-Dunlop, V. (1980) *A Handbook for Dance in Education.* Ester, Plymouth: MacDonald & Evans.

Radir, R. (1944) *Modern Dance For the Youth of America: A Text for High School and College Teachers.* New York: The Ronald Press Company.

Smith, J.M. (1976) *Dance Composition: A Practical Guide for Teachers.* London: Lepus.

Smith-Autard, J.M. (1994) *The Art of Dance in Education.* London: A & Black.

Spurgeon, D. (1991) *Dance Moves: From Improvisation to Dance.* Sydney: Harcourt Brace Jovanovich Publishers.

Stinson, S. (1988) *Dance for Young Children: Finding the Magic in Movement.* Virginia: The American Alliance for Health, Physical Educaton, Recreation and Dance.

Way, B. (1967) *Development through Drama.* London: Longman Group Ltd.

DOCUMENTS

National Arts Coalition Arts Education Task Group. (1994) Syllabus Proposals for the Creative Arts: Dance, Drama, Music, Visual Arts: Towards the provision of arts education in all schools in the Western Cape Province Region. Submitted to WESTAG.

Department of Education. (1995) Interim Core Syllabus: Dance – Creative Movement.

EIC & IEB. (1996) Understanding the National Qualifications Framework: A Guide to Lifelong Learning. Johannesburg: Heinemann Educational Publishers.

Western Cape Education Department. (1996) Continuous Asssessment – Communiqué, 1

Subject Index

Alphabetic Index